New Mexico
MAGAZINE

CENTENNIAL COOKBOOK

A CENTURY OF FLAVORS

EDITED BY MOLLY BOYLE AND LYNN CLINE

Photographs by Douglas Merriam

THE TEAM

Chief Executive Officer	Edward Graves
Editor in Chief	Steve Gleydura
Managing Editor	Kate Nelson
Senior Editor	Molly Boyle
Art & Photography Director	John McCauley
Assistant Art Director	Karin Eberhardt
Advertising & Special Projects Art Director	Terry Smith
Circulation Manager	Kurt Coey
Digital Manager	Ofelia Martinez

CONTRIBUTORS

Lynn Cline, Lois Ellen Frank, Cheryl Alters Jamison, Levi Romero, and Inez Russell Gomez

Contributing Copy Editors	Dianna Delling, Will Palmer
Finance Manager	Isabel B. López
Management Analyst Supervisor	Rayline Sebay
Management Analyst	Jalen Mayhew
Accountant/Auditor	Irania Veliz

Governor	Michelle Lujan Grisham
Tourism Department Secretary	Jen Paul Schroer
Tourism Deputy Secretary	Antoinette Vigil

ADVERTISING

Lianne Joy Aponte (505) 585-5569
lianne@nmmagazine.com
Northwestern and Northeastern NM (North of I-40), Santa Fe

Chris Romero (505) 670-1331
chris@nmmagazine.com
Southwestern and Southeastern NM (South of I-40)

First paperback edition 2023
By New Mexico Magazine

Copyright © 2023 by New Mexico Magazine
Published by New Mexico Magazine

ISBN 978-1-934480-28-1
Library of Congress Control Number: 2023905839

New Mexico Magazine
495 Old Santa Fe Trail
Santa Fe, New Mexico 87501

Designed by Karin Eberhardt
Cover photo by Douglas Merriam
Printed in Korea

New Mexico Magazine is an Enterprise Fund
of the State of New Mexico and is supported
by circulation, advertising, and sales revenues.

INTRODUCTION

From the first culinary story published in *New Mexico Magazine*—"Cookery as of Old," from February 1933—through the trove of articles and cookbooks we've produced since, America's oldest state magazine has invited readers to experience New Mexico's diverse and fascinating foodways.

We've told the evolving story of a unique cuisine steeped in ancient Indigenous and early Spanish traditions and seasoned with ingredients and techniques introduced by people from around the globe. The result is New Mexico cooking: a heady, gently simmering stew of local and multicultural flavors employed simply and creatively. One spoonful transports you to our corner of the world—and nowhere else.

"Everyone who has even a slight acquaintance with New Mexico knows the artistry and ingenuity of our cocineras," staffer Juliette C de Baca wrote in a 1966 *New Mexico Magazine* article. "Their skill comes from many generations of trial and error. And most of our recipes have been kitchen-tested for over 300 years!"

The *New Mexico Magazine Centennial Cookbook* brings that time-honored artistry to your kitchen, along with the earthy, spicy, and sweet flavors that make the Land of Enchantment one of the world's hottest culinary destinations. Across 50 enticing recipes drawn from the magazine's archives or shared by contemporary chefs throughout the state, we present an overgrown kitchen garden of histories, cuentos, cooking tips, and other fare. This journey of enchanting meals is guided by four essays from renowned New Mexico chefs and writers, who celebrate the glories of spring, summer, fall, and winter—because that's how we eat here. Season by season, we honor what the land provides.

We began by combing the magazine's archive for traditional recipes that have changed little over four centuries: staples such as red chile sauce, tortillas, and our famous chiles rellenos. We added classic dishes from pilgrimage-worthy restaurants, like Bar Castañeda's green chile smash burger, which pairs nicely with one of Sparky's frothy green chile milkshakes. We stirred in contemporary delights such as the Compound's apricot gazpacho, Cafe Pasqual's smoked trout hash, and the Pie-O-Neer's green chile and piñon apple pie. More tidbits come from the magazine's beloved food writers across the years, including Adela Amador, whose "Southwest Flavor" column was one of the most popular features of the 20th century.

Back to "Cookery as of Old," that very first food story: In it, Elizabeth Willis DeHuff reports that since all the dishes in New Mexico "are so distinctively a type of their own, in trying them out, one has a delightful feeling of daring and exhilaration." Though surely our chile plays a role in that rush, it's a fine description of what's been happening in New Mexico kitchens over the past 100 years. To many more!

—*Molly Boyle* and *Lynn Cline*, editors

**TAMALES
WITH RED CHILE
BEEF FILLING**

108

CONTENTS

T0028204

THE BUILDING BLOCKS OF NEW MEXICO FLAVORS

From New Mexico's cherished chile to the humble pinto bean slowly simmered to creamy perfection, ingredients grown in local soil have enhanced sauces, stews, and other traditional dishes for centuries. Recipes for our treasured tortillas, pillowy sopaipillas, earthy chicos, and other regional specialties have been handed down through generations, sustaining Ancestral Puebloans, Spanish settlers, cowboys and ranchers, homesteaders, and newcomers from across the globe. These recipes are the bedrock of New Mexico's extraordinary cuisine. ▧

The best recipes start with the best ingredients

GREEN CHILE SAUCE

The Original Owl Bar & Cafe is famous for its green chile cheeseburgers. The world-renowned Owl opened in 1945 in San Antonio, south of Socorro, and owes much of its reputation to this tasty green chile sauce, which has appeared in several *New Mexico Magazine* cookbooks. "The secret is in the simmering," says Rowena Baca, whose family has owned the restaurant for generations.

Makes approximately 12 servings

**3½ pounds hot green chile
  (or mild or medium, if that's
  your preference)**
1½ pounds ground beef
3 cloves garlic, minced
2 quarts water
Salt to taste

1. Roast, peel, and dice green chile.
2. In a heavy skillet, brown the meat and drain excess fat.
3. In a large, heavy saucepan, cover chile and garlic with water and bring to a boil. Mix in the meat and simmer, tightly covered, for at least 3 hours. Add salt to taste.

ROASTED FRESH GREEN CHILE

This simple method for preparing a batch of green chile appeared in our 1978 cookbook, *The Best from New Mexico Kitchens.* Nothing has changed since, save for the many new and delicious chile cultivars that have since been introduced to the state by the Chile Pepper Institute, at New Mexico State University.

Catch your green chiles—perhaps from the Mesilla or Española valleys, or around Chimayó. Rinse them, pat them dry, and don a pair of rubber gloves.

Slit pods lengthwise and remove seeds and veins. Place pods on a cookie sheet under a broiler, or place on an outdoor grill. (Put on goggles if you're working on a grill.) Allow pods to blister well on both sides. Turn frequently, using tongs, to avoid burning. Remove from fire and cover with a damp cloth or paper towels for 10 to 15 minutes. Then peel the skin from the stem downward. Chiles are ready to use in sauces, or to be chopped, bagged, and frozen for the future.

RED CHILE SAUCE

This simple sauce, a mainstay of traditional New Mexico cuisine and a returning champ from a few past magazine cookbooks, is referred to simply as "red" by locals. It's a foundation for enchiladas, tamales, carne adovada, and many other dishes. Cooks have been making it for centuries using dried whole pods, for concentrated flavor, or chile powder, which is quicker, easier, and equally delicious.

Makes approximately 2 cups

1 clove garlic, minced
3 tablespoons olive oil or lard
2 tablespoons flour
½ cup New Mexico red chile powder
2 cups water
Salt to taste

1. Sauté garlic in oil. Blend in flour with a wooden spoon. Add chile powder and blend. (Don't let the pan get too hot—chile will burn easily.)
2. Slowly add water and cook to desired consistency. Add salt to taste.

FLOUR TORTILLAS

Tortillas have been a culinary staple for thousands of years. According to a Maya legend, a peasant produced the first tortilla to feed his hungry king. You may feel like royalty when you taste the results of this recipe for perfectly fluffy flour tortillas from our October 2018 issue. It's inspired by the one that the tortilla masters use at Duran Central Pharmacy, in Albuquerque, where every tortilla has been rolled and cooked by hand for 80 years.

Makes 6 tortillas

2 cups flour
1 teaspoon baking powder
1 teaspoon salt
1 tablespoon lard or vegetable shortening
¾ cup lukewarm water

1. In a large mixing bowl, stir together the flour, baking powder, and salt, then add the lard or shortening. Work the fat into the flour with your hands until it resembles coarse bread crumbs. Add the water. Mix with your hands until it comes together into a sticky dough.

2. Gather the dough and turn it out onto a floured surface (the bowl works fine for the pros), kneading for about a minute, until it becomes smooth and satiny. Let it rest at least 15 minutes. Pinch off an egg-size ball. (Duran's tortillas are very big and very puffy, so their ball is the size of a turkey egg.) Shape the dough into a fat disk. Repeat with the remaining dough.

3. On a floured surface, give each disk a few quick passes with a roller, pressing from the center toward the edges. Give the dough a quarter turn and repeat until the circle is approximately ⅛-inch thick and 10 to 12 inches in diameter.

4. Heat a large cast-iron griddle or pan over high heat. Add one circle of dough and cook 30 to 45 seconds, until large bubbles form across the surface. Once brown spots have appeared on the bottom, flip the tortilla and cook another 30 to 45 seconds, until it puffs and browns on the other side. Rest the tortillas under a towel while you cook the others.

CORN TORTILLAS

For fresh corn tortillas, James Beard Award–winning cookbook author and former *New Mexico Magazine* contributing food editor Cheryl Alters Jamison recommends using tortilla-grind masa harina, or the finest grind a market sells. In this recipe, published in December 2013, she says that most cooks prefer to flatten the dough with an inexpensive tortilla press. These tortillas are best eaten fresh from the comal (a flat griddle).

Makes a dozen 5- to 6-inch tortillas

2 cups fine-ground white or yellow masa harina (a type of corn flour)
½ teaspoon salt
1¼ cups warm water, or more as needed

1. Mix ingredients with hands until dough is smooth—it should be quite moist but still hold its shape. Add a little more water or masa harina if needed to achieve proper consistency.
2. Form dough into 12 balls about 1½ inches in diameter. If not making tortillas immediately, cover balls with plastic wrap.
3. Heat dry griddle or heavy skillet over medium-high heat.
4. Place a ball of dough in the tortilla press between 2 sheets of plastic (sometimes sold with the press) or use a pair of sandwich- or quart-size plastic bags. Press ball until flattened to desired thickness, generally about ⅛ inch.
5. Carefully pull plastic from the round of dough and lay dough on hot griddle or comal. Cook tortilla 30 seconds, flip and cook for 1 minute on the other side, then flip it again to cook the first side another 30 seconds. Tortilla will be speckled with brown flecks.
6. Cover cooked tortillas to keep them warm while remaining balls of dough are shaped and cooked. Serve warm in basket with butter, chile, or salsa, or reserve for another dish.

CHICOS

Chicos are dried kernels of sweet corn that have been part of the Pueblo diet for centuries. Made from whole ears of corn traditionally steamed in the husk in an outdoor horno and then dried for days, chicos have a sensationally smoky, sweet flavor. Norma and Hutch Naranjo, who offer cooking classes at the Feasting Place from their house on Ohkay Owingeh Pueblo, introduce this uniquely New Mexican ingredient to their guests from around the world. "It's become a delicacy because of the long process of making chicos," says Norma, who shared this recipe for chicos, adapted

from her cookbook, *The Four Sisters: Keeping Family Traditions Alive* (2021). It's been passed down by her ancestors over hundreds of years. Don't have an horno? No problem —you can make this recipe using dried chicos sourced from New Mexico farmers.

Serves 6 to 10

1 pound dried chicos
2 to 2½ pounds stew meat (bison, short ribs or other beef, elk, venison, or pork), cubed
1 onion, diced
Garlic salt to taste

1. Cook chicos with 16 to 20 cups of water in large pot over medium heat for approximately 4 hours, until chicos are soft.
2. Meanwhile, brown meat in a large pot, then add onion and cook until translucent. Add 8 to 10 more cups of water and cook for 2½ hours, until meat is soft. Strain juice from meat-and-onion mixture and add mixture to chicos. Add garlic salt to taste.
3. Boil the meat mixture with the chicos for about 15 to 20 minutes, until the flavors marry.

FRIJOLES

Pinto beans are as much a part of New Mexico cuisine as our prized chile. In fact, both the pinto bean and the New Mexico chile are official state vegetables. (Never mind that chile is technically a fruit, and pinto beans are legumes.) None of that matters when you taste these creamy, aromatic frijoles pintos (Spanish for "painted bean"), a cherished dish in New Mexico. This recipe comes from Noe Canto, the longtime chef de cuisine at the Santa Fe School of Cooking. His frijoles are famous.

Serves 8 to 10

2 cups dry pinto beans, picked over for dirt or stones
2 tablespoons peanut oil or vegetable oil
1¼ cup onion, diced
1 tablespoon minced garlic
4 cups chicken broth or water, or a combination of the two
2 small bay leaves (optional)
1½ teaspoons dried Mexican oregano (optional)
1½ teaspoons dried epazote (optional)
1½ teaspoons ground cumin seed (optional)
½ teaspoon ground coriander seed (optional)
1 dried chipotle chile (optional)
1½ teaspoons sauce from a can of chipotles in adobo (optional)
1 teaspoon salt, or to taste

Overnight soaking helps to reduce the gaseous properties of the beans. If you choose to soak, drain and rinse the beans before starting the next phase.

1. Place the beans in a 6-quart pot. Cover with at least 3 inches of cold water, and bring to a boil. Reduce the heat and simmer for 2 to 3 hours, until they begin to soften. Drain and rinse well. (You can also cook in a pressure cooker.)

2. Heat the oil in a 6-quart pot over medium-high heat and sauté the onions until golden. Add the garlic and cook for 1 minute. Add the beans, broth, bay leaves, oregano, epazote, cumin, coriander, and dried chipotle and bring to a boil. Reduce the heat and simmer for approximately 1 hour, stirring frequently. Add more liquid if needed.

3. When the beans are creamy, add the canned chipotle sauce and the salt, then cook 15 minutes more. The beans should have enough liquid to stir easily.

IN PRAISE OF THE PINTO BEAN

"Though it be bitty, this bean stands tall. It's descended from one of the life-sustaining 'Three Sisters' of ancient Native cuisine, along with squash and corn. And it's one of the state's two official vegetables, even though it's technically a legume. (The other is chile, which is technically a fruit.) ...

"New Mexicans take their bean cooking seriously, and every cook has a preferred route: stovetop pot, pressure cooker, Crock-Pot, or even a micaceous clay pot. To pre or not to pre? (Soak, that is.) Add meat? Salt? Chile? There's no right answer. But if you consider yourself a fan of New Mexico fare, you need to master a method."

—*Kate Nelson, managing editor, from "The Bean That Fed the World," September 2019*

SOPAIPILLAS

Charlie Sandoval, of Charlie's Spic & Span Bakery & Cafe, in the original Las Vegas (the one in New Mexico), shares his family recipe for ethereally light and puffy sopaipillas. Since 1950, folks have gathered in this beloved downtown spot to fill up on sopaipillas, pastries, burritos, and other home-cooked delights, along with all the local gossip.

Makes 8 sopaipillas

4 cups flour

1 teaspoon salt

2 teaspoons baking powder

4 tablespoons lard or vegetable shortening

1½ cups warm water

4 cups vegetable or other oil, for frying

1. Put oil in Dutch oven and heat to 375°.
2. Whisk all dry ingredients in a bowl. Add lard or shortening until the mixture has a crumbly texture. Slowly add warm water and mix in stand mixer or by hand until a dough forms. (Make sure there aren't any lumps.)
3. Knead dough by hand or in mixer for about 2 minutes. Cover with a towel and let rest for about 20 minutes.
4. Flour your surface, then take dough ball and roll out with a rolling pin to ⅛- to ¼-inch thickness. Cut the dough into 8 even squares or triangles.
5. In batches, gently lay dough pieces into the fryer oil. Cook for about 1 minute, or until golden brown. During cooking, carefully spoon the hot oil on top of the exposed side of the dough; this will help it puff up. Flip sopaipilla to the other side and cook until golden.
6. Drain on paper towels and serve hot with honey, chile, or both (both is always best).

SOPAIPILLA VS. FRYBREAD

People often confuse sopaipillas and frybread as the same thing, but they are more like cousins, each a puffy fried dough with a prominent role in a distinctive hybrid cuisine. Sopaipillas are "heavenly bits of pastry," wrote *New Mexico Magazine* managing editor Kenneth Hardy in the March/April 1970 issue. They "are so fluffy that diners slather on either locally produced honey or homemade jam to keep them from floating off." These light and airy triangular pillows of dough, deep-fried to golden perfection, accompany many traditional meals in New Mexico, and are thought to have evolved from a similar fried dough originating in Spain.

FRYBREAD

Frybread is ubiquitous in New Mexico. A Native American staple, it provides the foundation for a Navajo taco, which is always on the menu at pow-wows, intertribal festivals, and many restaurants across the state. This basic recipe has appeared in several *New Mexico Magazine* cookbooks over the years.

Makes 6 to 8 frybreads

3 cups flour, either all white flour or half whole wheat flour
1½ teaspoons baking powder
½ teaspoon salt
1⅓ cups warm water
Shortening (lard is the traditional shortening, but you might prefer to use vegetable oil)

1. Mix flour, baking powder, and salt. Add warm water and mix. Dough should be soft but not sticky. Knead until smooth.
2. Tear off a chunk about the size of a peach. Pat and stretch until thin. Poke a hole in the middle and drop into sizzling-hot fat. Brown on both sides. Drain and serve hot with honey or jam.

Frybread is said to have been created by the Diné (Navajo) people after the U.S. government forced them to relocate from their homelands in Arizona and New Mexico to the Bosque Redondo internment camp at Fort Sumner, in eastern New Mexico, beginning in 1864. Unable to grow their traditional crops at the camp, the Diné were given rations by the U.S. government, which included previously unfamiliar ingredients such as lard, white flour, and processed sugar. At Bosque Redondo, they turned those ingredients into frybread, which has become

PLANTING SEEDS, HONORING GENERATIONS

BY LOIS ELLEN FRANK, PH.D.

Spring is a time of renewal. In this season, for millennia, Native American farmers have always begun to prepare the ground and land for the gardens that will grow throughout the summer and be ready to harvest in the fall. Spring is representative of new growth and a time to plan which crops to plant, to prepare seeds, and to begin the new growing season. →

Savor
the Flavors
of
the Seasons
at a
New Mexico
Bed &
Breakfast

Every spring, I decide what chiles and how many kinds of tomatoes I will plant, and I plan where I will plant the Three Sisters—corn, beans, and squash. This Native American triad, famous for how well they grow together in the garden, represents the interconnectedness they share, and the Three Sisters are considered gifts from the Great Spirit by some Native communities. Corn needs nitrogen to grow, and beans provide nitrogen to the soil; squash, with its big leaves, provides shade to the soil and prevents weed growth; corn provides a support for the beans to climb. Indigenous understanding of sustainability is based on the philosophy that all things are integrally connected.

In New Mexico, Native communities often say that a healthy environment means a healthy culture, which means a healthy people. The people here have numerous ways of planting these ancestral foods. Some of the oldest sustainable farming methods in the Southwest include terrace gardening, a type of farming used on hillsides; dry farming, using water runoff from the summer monsoon rains; and, on a smaller scale, waffle gardening, which uses square sunken garden beds enclosed by clay walls that create waffle-like shapes. These squares hold the water around each plant to ensure their growth. The Zuni are famous for using this method of gardening, which dates back thousands of years. Today these gardening techniques are still practiced, and a growing number of people all over the Southwest are adopting this traditional farming practice.

The Three Sisters are among the cultivars that form the foundation of New Mexican cuisine. Many of these ingredients star in dishes we enjoy today, including posole, cornmeal-based breads, puddings, atole, hotcakes, soups and stews, and a variety of corn, bean, squash, chile, and tomato recipes. Since spring is the beginning of the growing cycle, traditionally the dishes prepared during this time include dried ingredients harvested the year before.

I am passionate about cooking with ancestral Native American ingredients and educating people on the intersection of food and culture. I cook with Native chef Walter Whitewater (Diné) at my catering company, Red Mesa Cuisine, and we believe food has a story of how it nurtured the ancestors and sustained generations. Many people are unaware of the contributions that Native people have made to the foods that we eat today, including corn, beans, squash, chiles, tomatoes, potatoes, vanilla, and cacao, which I call the Magic Eight. Yet when we prepare these foods, we revitalize everything associated with them. And when we feed people, we nurture them while honoring the ancestors. 🍃

> IN NEW MEXICO, NATIVE COMMUNITIES OFTEN SAY THAT A HEALTHY ENVIRONMENT MEANS A HEALTHY CULTURE, WHICH MEANS A HEALTHY PEOPLE.

LOIS ELLEN FRANK *is a Santa Fe-based chef, Native American foods historian, culinary anthropologist, educator, photographer, organic gardener, and James Beard Award–winning cookbook author. She is the chef-owner of Red Mesa Cuisine, a catering company specializing in Indigenous cuisine and cultural education. Frank has spent more than 30 years documenting and working with the foods and lifeways of Native American communities in the Southwest.*

SMOKED TROUT HASH (WITH) POACHED EGGS (AND) TOMATILLO SALSA

Katharine Kagel opened Cafe Pasqual's in 1979, blazing a trail that helped establish Santa Fe as a culinary capital. Named after the patron saint of cooks and kitchens and honored with the James Beard Foundation's America's Classics award, Cafe Pasqual's is known for delightfully fresh food, such as this perennially popular breakfast dish that appeared in our July 2017 issue and in *Cooking with Cafe Pasqual's* (Ten Speed Press, 2006). It stimulates every part of the palate, Kagel says, "salty, sweet, and zesty all at once." It's also a great way to prepare the trout you snagged while fishing in a New Mexico river, lake, or mountain stream.

Serves 4

TOMATILLO SALSA

10 large tomatillos, husked and rinsed
1 to 2 jalapeños, stemmed and halved
¼ white onion, coarsely chopped
1 clove garlic
20 sprigs cilantro, including stems
1 to 2 chiles de árbol, stemmed
2 cups tightly packed spinach leaves
1½ teaspoons kosher salt

1. Put all the ingredients into the container of a blender. Whirl until liquefied. Taste for heat and add more chiles if desired. Transfer to a serving bowl.

HASH BROWN POTATO CAKES

4 russet baking potatoes (2 pounds), peeled
1 cup grated Gruyère cheese
¼ cup finely minced fresh chives
1½ teaspoons kosher salt
1½ teaspoons freshly ground black pepper
4 tablespoons (½ stick) butter

1. To make the potato cakes, in a large stockpot, bring to a boil enough water to cover the potatoes. Add the potatoes and cook for 20 minutes at high heat, or until a fork piercing the potato just slips in. (Do not overcook.) Drain the water and let the potatoes cool completely. This may take as long as 3 hours. You may want to make the potatoes a day in advance and refrigerate them, because they need to be absolutely cool for grating.

2. Grate the potatoes on a hand grater. In a large bowl, mix the potatoes, cheese, chives, salt, and pepper, gently lifting and tossing the ingredients with your hands.

3. Preheat the oven to 200°. Put 1 tablespoon of the butter into a preheated 7-inch nonstick skillet and allow the butter to cover the pan. When the butter is heated, hand-pat one-fourth of the potato mixture into the pan. Sauté the potatoes over medium-high heat, 3 to 4 minutes per side, or until golden. Repeat for the remaining 3 potato pancakes. Keep the potato cakes warm in the oven until the whole dish is ready for assembly.

4. Preheat 4 plates.

POACHED EGGS

2 tablespoons white vinegar
8 large eggs

1. Poach the eggs by filling a 12-inch straight-sided nonreactive sauté pan with water until three-fourths filled, and then add white vinegar. The addition of vinegar helps ensure that the eggs will remain egg-shaped and that the whites will not stream about the pan. Place the skillet over high heat. Crack an egg one at a time into a shallow bowl, and when the water is simmering, slip the egg into the water.

2. Repeat, cooking the eggs in 2 batches of 4 eggs each. Cook the eggs for 4 to 5 minutes, until the whites are firm but the yolks are still soft inside.

ASSEMBLY

1 tablespoon butter
1 pound smoked trout, torn into 3-by-1-inch pieces
Parsley or cilantro sprigs for garnish

1. While the eggs are cooking, begin to assemble the dish. Place the potato pancakes on the warmed plates. Put the tablespoon of butter in a sauté pan, add the trout, and heat through, about 1 minute on each side.

2. When the eggs are opaque in appearance, lift them out of the water with a slotted spoon, letting them drain over the pan. Place 2 poached eggs on top of each of the potato pancakes. Gently dab the top of each egg with a kitchen towel or paper towel to dry the eggs so that the tomatillo salsa will not slide off. Spoon 2 tablespoons of tomatillo salsa over the eggs and scatter the trout around the potato pancake. Serve the remaining salsa in a bowl for those who may want more. Garnish with parsley or cilantro sprigs.

QUELITES

A traditional New Mexico specialty that is especially popular during Lent, quelites taste best when made with wild spinach (lamb's quarters) or purslane, which grow abundantly in many backyards and fields throughout the state. But you can do well using the "tame" kind of spinach. Some traditional recipes for quelites call for stirring a few tablespoons of cooked beans, peas, or lentils into the spinach just before serving.

Serves 2 to 3

½ pound fresh wild spinach
1 tablespoon shortening or oil
3 tablespoons onion, chopped
1 tablespoon sweet peas
¼ teaspoon crushed red chile
Salt to taste

1. Wash greens well, chop, and steam for about 10 minutes, or until tender.
2. Sauté the onion in shortening, mix in drained spinach, chile, peas, and salt, and cook for an additional 5 minutes.

THE POWER OF PLANTS

Traditional plants are deeply rooted in New Mexico culture, used for medicinal and culinary purposes by Ancestral Puebloans, Spanish settlers, mountain men, homesteaders, and many others who made the region their home. New Mexico herbs include oshá, a member of the parsley family that Native people have harvested for centuries to help ease cold symptoms and respiratory problems. The root can be chewed or made into a tea. Chokecherry has long been prized for its antioxidant-rich juice, extracted from the shrub's dark red berries and used to make tasty jellies, syrups, sauces, and liqueurs. The ancient Pueblo people knew that a tea made from chokecherry bark was a remedy for everything from headaches to heart problems. Cota, or Navajo tea, is wild-harvested by Diné and Zuni people as plant medicine for a variety of ailments. When Spanish colonists arrived in the 16th century, they brought with them Mediterranean herbs—lavender, oregano, and sweet basil, which New Mexicans cooked with and also carried in their pockets for luck. Even anise, whose dried seeds give New Mexico's bizcochitos their lovely licorice-like flavor, serves a dual purpose, being a remedy for indigestion.

ORANGE, JICAMA, AND PEPPER SALAD WITH RED CHILE VINAIGRETTE

Published in our November 2012 issue, this dish makes for an unusual use of chile. It's tangy and refreshing, it brings color to the table, and the earthy red chile adds a slight heat. Spoon the salad on a butter lettuce leaf and serve with tortilla triangles. For an especially colorful presentation, use blood oranges.

Serves 8

DRESSING

¼ cup rice vinegar
1 teaspoon chopped fresh ginger
2 tablespoons orange juice
1 teaspoon red chile powder, plus
    more for garnish (optional)
¾ cup extra virgin olive oil

SALAD

4 cups orange, blood orange, or mandarin orange slices
2 cups julienne-sliced jicama (1½-inch strips)
1 cup julienne-sliced red bell pepper (1½-inch strips)
1 cup julienne-sliced green pepper (1½-inch strips)
8 butter lettuce leaves
Tortilla chips
Red chile powder, for optional garnish

1. In a mixing bowl, combine the rice vinegar, ginger, orange juice, and red chile. Slowly whisk the olive oil into the mixture until it is incorporated. This mixture can be refrigerated for about 1 week.
2. Toss the oranges, jicama, and bell peppers with the vinaigrette. Place about ½ cup of the fruit mixture into the lettuce leaf. Sprinkle with red chile powder if desired.

BEANS, GREENS, AND BLUE CORN MUFFINS

These recipes are FARMesilla chef Becky Windels's ode to her mother and father, who were excellent home cooks. At the FARMesilla farm store and café, in Mesilla, near Las Cruces, diners can't get enough of this dish. Traditionally prepared with pinto beans, ham hocks, turnip or collard greens, and sweet cornbread, this combo was a staple at every family gathering. Windels created this lightened-up version with a spicy twist. While each of the five parts is vegetarian and gluten-free, you can easily add bacon or any other protein you desire.

Serves 4 to 6, with delicious leftovers

SMOKY PINTO BEANS IN CHILE MORITA SALSA VERDE

1½ cups New Mexico pinto beans (take care to sort and thoroughly rinse)
3½ cups water
3 cups chile morita salsa verde (recipe follows)
2 teaspoons sea salt

1. Place pinto beans and cold filtered water in the pot of a pressure cooker (an Instant Pot will work). Pressure-cook on high, set for 52 minutes. When cook time is finished, place a dish cloth over vent and manually release. When pressure is fully released, stir in chile morita salsa verde (see next step) and sea salt. Add 1 additional cup of water. Simmer on low for 8 to 10 minutes to allow flavors to mingle. Set on warm until ready to serve.
2. While beans are cooking, prepare the chile morita salsa verde.

CHILE MORITA SALSA VERDE

Makes 7 cups

Morita chiles are a type of chipotle pepper— a smoked, dried version of red jalapeños. Chipotle would be a good substitute, but Windels prefers the dark, smoky flavor of this variety.

6 whole morita chiles, stemmed and seeded
1¼ pounds tomatillos, peeled and rinsed
2 tablespoons Dry Point Distillers or other bourbon
1 garlic clove, smashed
1 cup low-salt vegetable or chicken stock
1 teaspoon sea salt

1. Soak the morita chiles in hot water until soft and pliable (about 20 minutes). In a blender, puree chiles until smooth, adding just enough of the chile water to make a paste. Set aside.
2. Preheat oven to 400°. To char-roast salsa, place tomatillos, bourbon, garlic, stock,

and salt in a cast-iron skillet and bake for 30 minutes. A good char on the tomatillo is what you are looking for. Remove and let cool.

3. Add 1 tablespoon chile morita puree. (Add more puree if you prefer a hotter salsa.) Adjust seasoning to taste. In a blender or food processor, pulse the cooled tomatillo/morita mixture; you want it chunky for your beans.

CHILE- AND LIME-SPICED CRISP KALE

Choose New Mexico–grown kale at the farmers' market if available. Curly varieties work best here.

1 bunch red kale, rinsed, dried, stems removed
1 bunch green kale, rinsed, dried, stems removed
Olive oil–based pan spray
Chile-lime spice, such as Tajín

1. Set oven to 335°. Spread out kale leaves in a single layer on sheet pans. (You may need to cook in 3 or 4 batches.) Gently coat all leaves with olive oil spray. Bake each pan for 10 to 12 minutes; have a spatula nearby and turn over each leaf halfway through baking time. Remove the crisped leaves onto sheet tray lined with a cooling rack. If any leaves are still wilted, return them to the oven for another 1 to 2 minutes. Dust with chile-lime spice.

HIBISCUS PICKLED RED ONIONS

Make this the day before serving; it takes 24 hours to turn a beautiful bright pink.

½ cup red wine vinegar
½ cup freshly squeezed lime juice
½ cup water
¼ cup palm sugar
½ tablespoon sea salt
¼ cup dried hibiscus flowers
1 to 2 New Mexico–grown red onions, thinly sliced into half-moons
1 small to medium red beet, rinsed and scrubbed (no need to peel; you will discard)

1. Simmer first six ingredients to dissolve for approximately 5 minutes. Using a fine mesh strainer, strain and discard hibiscus.
2. Place sliced red onion in a heatproof container. Layer 1 small beet in between the onions, finishing with a few on top. Pour hot solution over vegetables to be pickled. Top with a plate to keep onions and beets submerged. Cover and chill overnight.
3. The next day, discard beets. Pickled onions will last 1 to 2 weeks, refrigerated.

BLUE CORN MUFFINS

DRY MIX

1¼ cup blue cornmeal (FARMesilla uses
 Tamaya Blue cornmeal from Santa Ana
 Pueblo)
1¼ cup gluten-free flour
⅔ cup palm sugar
1½ teaspoons sea salt
1 tablespoon baking powder
1 teaspoon baking soda

WET MIX

2 large cage-free eggs
1 pint plain yogurt
½ cup sunflower or avocado oil

1. Place dry mix in a mixing bowl. Add wet
   ingredients; whisk until combined. Let
   batter set for a minimum of 8 hours,
   preferably overnight.*
2. When ready to bake, preheat oven to
   400° with convection fan on. Prepare a
   12-muffin pan with cooking spray. Divide
   batter evenly. Bake 16 minutes, rotating
   pan halfway through.

*Allowing the coarse blue corn to set with the
acidity in the yogurt overnight both softens
the blue corn and results in a deep-blue corn
muffin. We have tried finer grains but found
they turned out dense as opposed to fluffy
and cakey, like we like it.*

ASSEMBLY

3–4 ounces queso fresco, crumbled
Butter
Scallions or chives
Hot sauce

1. Ladle 8 to 10 ounces of warm pinto beans
   into a bowl.
2. Top with drained pickled red onions, a
   high stack of crispy kale, and crumbled
   queso fresco.
3. Serve with a warm blue corn muffin
   topped with butter and scallions or chives,
   and hot sauce on the side

GREEN CHILE LAMB OSSO BUCO

Lambs are born in the spring, and their tender meat is a popular entrée on Easter and Passover tables. This recipe from the April 2022 *New Mexico Magazine*, by contributor Chef Johnny Vee, director of Las Cosas Cooking School, in Santa Fe, offers a creative take on osso buco (Italian for "bone with a hole"), which is traditionally made with veal shanks. He finds that replacing the veal with lamb shanks makes a much tastier dish. Green chile also elevates the flavor. This dish is great for entertaining, because you can cook it completely, then rewarm when you're ready to serve, preferably with a potato side dish or wild mushroom risotto.

Serves 4

2 teaspoons kosher salt, divided
2 teaspoons freshly ground
**   black pepper, divided**
½ cup flour
4 lamb shanks, approximately
**   10 ounces each**
4 tablespoons olive oil
4 garlic cloves, minced
1 large yellow onion, diced
1 cup mushrooms, quartered
2 tablespoons fresh thyme leaves
1 14½-ounce can diced tomatoes,
**   with their liquid**
4 cups chicken stock
1 cup dry red wine like merlot
**   or cabernet**
1 to 2 bay leaves
1 cup New Mexico green chile
**   (mild, medium, or hot),**
**   roasted, peeled, seeded,**
**   and chopped**
Sprigs of parsley

1. Mix 1 teaspoon salt and 1 teaspoon pepper together with the flour, then dust the shanks on all sides.

2. Place olive oil in heavy-bottomed Dutch oven or roasting pan and brown shanks on all sides over medium to medium-high heat. Remove shanks from Dutch oven or pan and set aside.

3. With the pan on medium, add garlic, onion, and mushrooms. Sauté until onion starts to brown.

4. Add thyme, tomatoes, stock, and wine. Allow liquid to come to a boil. Stir in remaining salt and pepper, bay leaves, and green chile. Nestle the shanks into the sauce; they may not be completely covered with liquid, but that's fine.

5. Cover Dutch oven or pan, place in preheated 400° oven, and cook for approximately 2½ hours. The dish is done when the shanks are very tender and almost falling off the bone. Serve in a bowl with gravy ladled over it, topped with parsley.

COWBOY STEAK ⬤WITH RED CHILE ONION RINGS

When Mark Miller opened Coyote Cafe in 1987, his pioneering modern Southwestern cuisine made Santa Fe an international dining destination. Blending ancient culinary traditions with contemporary techniques, he transformed regional ingredients into dazzling, innovative dishes. Miller sold his legendary restaurant years ago, but it endures as a Santa Fe classic. This hearty steak, paired with red-chile-dusted onion rings, remains a star of modern Southwestern cuisine and of our March 2018 issue.

Serves 4

4 prime bone-in rib-eye steaks, or other high-quality bone-in rib-eye steaks, cut 1½ inches thick

4 white onions, cut into rings no more than ⅛ inch thick (use a mandoline for even thinner ones)

3 cups whole milk

3 cups all-purpose flour

½ cup ground dried New Mexico red chile

2 tablespoons plus 2 teaspoons cornstarch

1 tablespoon kosher salt

1 teaspoon ground cumin

2 teaspoons granulated sugar

2 teaspoons hot Spanish paprika

Vegetable oil for deep-frying

Kosher salt and freshly ground pepper

1. Let steaks sit at room temperature for about 1 hour. Soak onions in milk in a large bowl for 1 hour.

2. Heat oven to 300°. In a medium bowl, mix flour, chile, cornstarch, salt, cumin, sugar, and paprika. Drain onions, then dredge in flour mixture. Heat at least 4 inches of oil in a large, heavy saucepan to 360°. Add onions in batches and cook until golden brown, about 45 seconds. Transfer with tongs or a large slotted spoon to paper towels, then transfer, in a thin layer, to a baking sheet and keep warm in the oven.

3. Season steaks generously with salt and pepper. Heat two large cast-iron skillets over medium-high heat for several minutes. Add steaks. Cook to desired doneness, about 7 minutes per side for medium rare, pouring off excess fat before turning. Transfer to plates, scatter with onion rings, and serve immediately.

FRITO PIE

In the small northern New Mexico community of El Rito, El Farolito has served phenomenal New Mexican food for more than four decades. This mom-and-pop eatery has earned praise from *Gourmet*, *Travel + Leisure*, and other major magazines. An excellent portable companion often sold at high school athletic games, Frito pies are best served in the traditional fashion, playfully stuffed inside an individual-size Fritos bag.

Serves 4

1 pound ground beef
4 cups Fritos corn chips
2 cups cooked pinto
   beans
2 cups red chile sauce
2 chopped onions

1 cup shredded lettuce
1 cup diced tomato
2 cups grated cheddar
   cheese

1. Sauté ground beef in a skillet over medium heat. Drain and set aside until ready to use.
2. Stir red chile sauce into ground beef.
3. Place a handful of Frito chips in a bowl (or keep them in their bag) and top with ground beef-chile mixture and pinto beans. Garnish with onions, lettuce, tomato, and cheese.

THE FRITO PIE FLAP

Who invented the world-famous Frito pie, and where? It all depends on whom you ask. In Texas, home to the Frito-Lay company, Kaleta Doolin, daughter of Fritos founder Charles Doolin, says that her mother created the dish in 1932, when she poured a can of chili over the family's corn chips. In New Mexico, a different story credits Teresa Hernández, a cook at the Woolworths lunch counter on the Santa Fe Plaza (now the Five & Dime general store), for inventing the recipe in the 1960s. This controversy pales in comparison with the food fight started by Anthony Bourdain when he insulted the Frito pie during a 2013 visit to Santa Fe to film his *Parts Unknown* TV show. He inaccurately stated that the cherished dish was made with "canned Hormel chili and a Day-Glo-orange cheese-like substance." His insults went viral. New Mexicans were outraged, and Bourdain, realizing his blunder, apologized.

CAPIROTADA

Also called sopa, this traditional Lenten dish provides a way to use stale bread. With the addition of sugar and spices, capirotada makes a delicious dessert. Most New Mexicans have their own version of this popular dish, which is a great way to use local nuts. This recipe is from Adela Amador's cookbook, *Southwest Flavor: Adela Amador's Tales from the Kitchen—Recipes and Stories from New Mexico Magazine.*

Serves 6 to 8

14 slices of bread (any kind)
½ cup piñon nuts, pecans, or peanuts, chopped
2 cups sugar
3 ½ cups water
1 cup raisins
1½ teaspoons vanilla
1 teaspoon cinnamon
5 tablespoons butter
½ cup sweet wine (optional)
1 cup shredded cheese (Jack or longhorn)
1 cup whipped cream for garnish

1. Butter ovenproof baking dish.
2. Tear bread into 1-inch pieces and toast in 350° oven for 10 minutes.
3. Toss bread and nuts in mixing bowl.
4. Place sugar in saucepan over medium heat and stir continuously until sugar melts and turns a caramel color.
5. Add water immediately, being very careful, because the syrup will bubble and splatter. Caramel might partially solidify but will liquefy as it reheats.
6. Reduce heat and stir raisins, vanilla, cinnamon, and butter into caramel syrup while still hot.
7. Stir until butter melts, then pour syrup mixture over bread mixture. If not entirely soaked, add sweet wine as needed.
8. Place mixture in baking dish and top with cheese.
9. Bake at 350° for 30 minutes.
10. Serve with whipped cream or ice cream.

LAVENDER POUND CAKE

New Mexico's arid, sunny climate is ideal for growing lavender. The fragrant flowering plant flourishes throughout the state, in private gardens and on lavender farms like Los Poblanos Historic Inn & Organic Farm, in Los Ranchos de Albuquerque, and Purple Adobe Lavender Farm, in Abiquiú. This recipe from Los Poblanos, published in several *New Mexico Magazine* cookbooks, makes a perfect treat for a late-spring picnic. Take care to use only culinary lavender; others can taste soapy. English lavender (*Lavandula angustifolia*) is a chefs' favorite.

Makes 1 loaf

1¼ cups (2½ sticks) butter (room temperature)
1½ cups sugar
¾ teaspoon vanilla
6 eggs
¾ teaspoon salt
2⅔ cups white flour
2 tablespoons culinary lavender petals
Lavender syrup (recipe right)
Mint leaves for garnish

1. Preheat oven to 325°. Cream butter and sugar. Stir in vanilla and eggs and, when smooth, add salt, flour, and lavender petals until just combined.
2. Pour batter into a prepared loaf pan and bake for about 1 hour. If cake is getting too dark on top, turn the oven down to 300°.
3. Cool for 10 minutes in pan, then remove and brush top and sides with lavender syrup while cake is still warm. Garnish with mint leaves.

LAVENDER SYRUP

1 cup water
1 cup sugar
½ cup culinary lavender petals

1. Bring water and sugar to a boil. Once sugar has dissolved, remove from heat and stir in lavender petals.
2. Let cool to room temperature, then transfer to an airtight container.
3. Chill overnight, then strain. Syrup will keep for 2 months in refrigerator.

CUCUMBER–JALAPEÑO MARGARITA

Since 1939, La Posta de Mesilla has served tasty New Mexican food made from century-old family recipes in a 150-year-old adobe that's listed on the National Register of Historic Places. Across the decades, La Posta also has been the place to go for innovative margaritas, including this one, rimmed with New Mexico pecans grown in the Mesilla Valley. "This drink epitomizes the harvest of the Mesilla Valley—Hatch-grown jalapeños and green chile, Mesilla Valley pecans, and local honey," says Jerean Camuñez Hutchinson, great-niece of La Posta founder Katy Griggs. As co-owners, she and her husband continue the legacy of this long-lauded restaurant.

Makes 1 margarita

3 cucumber wheels, peeled
2 to 3 jalapeño wheels, depending
   on heat tolerance
1 ounce fresh lime juice
1¼ ounces agave syrup
1½ ounces 100-percent agave
   silver/blanco tequila
Local honey, green chile salt, and
   chopped pecans for glass rim

1. In a mixing glass, muddle 2 of the cucumber wheels, 1 to 2 jalapeño wheels, fresh lime juice, and agave nectar. Add tequila and ice. Shake vigorously and pour into an ice-filled margarita glass that's been rimmed with local honey and dipped upside down in a mixture of green chile salt and chopped pecans. Garnish with cucumber and jalapeño wheels dropped in the glass.

THE BOUNTY OF SUMMER

BY CHERYL ALTERS JAMISON

I love summer, with its procession of stone fruits, ripe and juicy, from cherries to apricots to plums and peaches. They fill pies, crisps, and cobblers. They're swirled into ice creams, sometimes with later-season blackberries and raspberries. The spring asparagus and quelites yield to summer squash and corn, with pinto and bolita beans twining up the stalks. Tomatoes ripen in a profusion of colors and shapes, begging to be eaten with a shake of salt over the sink, or maybe layered on a platter or in the best BLT of the year. →

Mindful flavor.

santafe
COUNTY

NM
TRUE

SantaFeNMTrue.com

The cool crispness of cucumbers, from long slicers to small pickling cukes, makes a welcome antidote to hot days, especially when paired with feathery fronds of dill. Toward summer's climax, our signature green chile blankets the state.

Sure, that chile will mature to an even flashier red in a few weeks' time, but the emerald pods own the month of August. They need the steady heat of high summer to mature. Chiles can be plucked from their bushy plants and combined with that summer squash and corn to make our perennially popular seasonal dish calabacitas. Sure, the dish's name means "little squashes," but it would be nothing without the supporting pops of heat, color, and flavor that the green chile provides. Fresh green covers enchiladas and burritos, of course, but it makes its way into all manner of other dishes. Find it exuberantly topping a pizza, livening up sushi or tuna salad, or zipping up the frosting on a cupcake. It's all fleeting, but oh, what a summer fling.

This seasonal New Mexican bounty is some kind of miracle. Summer's blistering sunshine isn't far removed from spring's last frost, and at the other end of summer, the killer cold might come to high mountain valleys well before Labor Day. We have only one major río running through the state, and while it's grande in name, much of it is claimed for other needs besides farming. The weather can be unrelentingly dry. Until it isn't.

Midsummer's fearsome monsoons can wash away young plants. Often, the soil is more effective as a building material than a planting medium. It sounds like a recipe for disaster. However, the challenges mean that our state's agriculture has stayed small-scale, with very little of the industrial agribusiness that often pollutes land and takes money out of farmers' pockets.

Ultimately, that's a very good thing. It means we have a wonderful network of small farmers concerned with sustainably grown, fully flavored fruits and vegetables, and markets throughout the state where folks can buy all that produce direct from the grower.

Miraculous indeed. Embrace the fleeting season. 🔥

> THIS SEASONAL NEW MEXICAN BOUNTY IS SOME KIND OF MIRACLE. SUMMER'S BLISTERING SUNSHINE ISN'T FAR REMOVED FROM SPRING'S LAST FROST, AND AT THE OTHER END OF SUMMER, THE KILLER COLD MIGHT COME TO HIGH MOUNTAIN VALLEYS WELL BEFORE LABOR DAY.

CHERYL ALTERS JAMISON *is a four-time James Beard Award–winning cookbook author, whose books include* Tasting New Mexico *and* The Rancho de Chimayó Cookbook, *and a former contributing culinary editor for* New Mexico Magazine. *She lives in a renovated 100-year-old dairy barn in Tesuque, where she raises a small flock of chickens.*

GEORGIA O'KEEFFE'S APRICOT MUFFINS

When she wasn't in her studio, iconic American artist Georgia O'Keeffe enjoyed her Abiquiú garden, where she grew green chile, squash, tomatoes, herbs, and other fresh fare. Her fruit trees produced pears, apples, and apricots, which provided the inspiration for this recipe created by Margaret Wood, an assistant and personal chef for O'Keeffe. Wood wrote about their time together in *A Painter's Kitchen: Recipes from the Kitchen of Georgia O'Keeffe*. In April 2017, we excerpted this recipe for healthy, mouth-watering muffins.

Makes 1 dozen muffins

¼ cup dried apricots
1 cup whole wheat flour
¼ cup raw wheat germ
1 tablespoon baking powder
¼ teaspoon salt
¼ cup pecans, roughly chopped
1 egg
1 cup yogurt
2 tablespoons honey, or to taste
¼ cup oil

1. Cover the dried apricots with boiling water. Let stand at least 30 minutes.
2. Meanwhile, combine the flour, wheat germ, baking powder, salt, and pecans in a large mixing bowl.
3. In a smaller bowl, beat the egg, then add the yogurt, honey, and oil. When the apricots are soft, roughly chop them.
4. Add the wet ingredients and the chopped apricots to the dry ingredients. Mix only until slightly blended.
5. Preheat the oven to 400°. Grease a muffin tin and pour the batter so that each cup is half full. Bake muffins for 20 to 25 minutes, or until browned. Serve with butter and fruit preserves, if desired.

From *A Painter's Kitchen: Recipes from the Kitchen of Georgia O'Keeffe* (MNMP, © 2009 by Margaret Wood)

FIESTA SALSA

Gather friends and family around a fresh bowl of satisfying salsa and you've got the ingredients for a lively summer get-together, especially with this zesty recipe by Lynn Nusom, who wrote many books on Southwestern and New Mexican history and cuisine. He contributed this recipe to *New Mexico Magazine* in March 1996.

Makes approximately 2½ cups

4 large, firm red tomatoes, briefly run under
    hot water, peeled, and coarsely chopped
4 tomatillos, husks removed, finely chopped
1 medium yellow onion, peeled and diced
3 New Mexico green chiles, such as Big Jim or
    Sandía, roasted, peeled, and seeded
1 jalapeño, seeds and membranes removed,
    finely diced
2 cloves garlic, peeled and finely chopped
3 tablespoons white wine vinegar
1 tablespoon fresh cilantro leaves, finely
    chopped
1 teaspoon ground black pepper
½ teaspoon salt
½ teaspoon dried oregano, crushed

1. Mix all ingredients together and chill in the refrigerator for 1 hour before serving.
2. Serve with tortilla chips or as a side dish with grilled steaks or chicken.

CHILLED APRICOT GAZPACHO

For more than 55 years, the Compound restaurant, in Santa Fe, has served exquisite contemporary American food in a setting where legendary designer Alexander Girard blended folk art and midcentury-modern influences. This recipe, from executive chef Weston Ludeke, exemplifies the restaurant's approach to local ingredients—in this case, apricots, which are in season every summer for only about three weeks. "I love to use them everywhere I can for as long as I can," Ludeke says. "Of course, a few days after buying the fruit, the sugars start to turn and the texture is less desirable. What I love about this gazpacho is that it allows you to savor the flavors of the apricots in a different way, while using every piece of fruit you have. I suggest saving this recipe for when you have over-ripened fruit, not allowing any of the short season to go to waste."

Serves 4

GAZPACHO

6 ripe apricots, pitted and quartered
2 Roma tomatoes, seeds removed
1 large English cucumber, peeled, seeded, and roughly chopped
1 clove garlic, roughly chopped
½ red onion, thinly sliced
¼ cup sherry vinegar (can substitute red wine vinegar)
½ cup extra virgin olive oil
2 cups vegetable stock
3 tablespoons salt

WHIPPED FETA CHEESE

4 ounces feta cheese
2 ounces crème fraîche (or substitute sour cream)
1 lemon, zested and juiced

GRILLED APRICOTS

2 apricots, pitted and halved
Pinch of salt
Dash of olive oil

Sumac powder for garnish
Chopped mint for garnish

1. Make gazpacho: Place apricots and all vegetables, vinegar, olive oil, stock, and salt in a large lock-tight container and marinate overnight, or for a minimum of 4 hours if pressed for time.

2. Blend all together in blender until smooth consistency. Immediately chill and reserve for serving.

3. Make whipped feta: Place feta cheese, crème fraîche, and lemon juice in a food processor and pulse until blended. Transfer to a bowl and fold in lemon zest. Chill and reserve for serving.

4. Grill apricots: Toss apricot halves with a pinch of salt and olive oil and grill over high heat until marked. (You can also use a cast-iron pan.) This should be quick, so as not to cook the fruit but just bring some grilled flavor to the dish. Cool, then dice.

5. To serve, place whipped feta cheese in the center of a plate and top with a grilled, diced apricot half. Garnish with sumac powder and chopped mint. Pour gazpacho evenly across four bowls and enjoy.

CALABACITAS

"Little squashes," one of New Mexico's most enduring dishes, have been made in various ways over the centuries, but summer squash is usually the essential ingredient. Many cooks scatter ⅓ cup of grated pepper Jack cheese over the dish just before serving. You can also use the dish to stuff tamales or chiles rellenos if you chop the squash into smaller pieces. This recipe from Chef Johnny Vee comes from our October 2021 issue.

Serves 8

2 tablespoons olive oil
1 medium red onion, chopped in ¼-inch dice
3 garlic cloves, minced
3 zucchini, halved lengthwise and cut crosswise in ½-inch slices
3 yellow squash, halved lengthwise and cut crosswise in ½-inch slices
3 New Mexico green chiles, roasted, peeled, seeded, and chopped
3 ears of corn, shucked and kernels sliced off
¼ teaspoon ground cumin, toasted
½ teaspoon Mexican oregano
½ cup vegetable stock
Salt and pepper to taste

1. Heat olive oil in heavy Dutch oven and sauté onion over medium heat until translucent, about 5 minutes. Add garlic and sauté until lightly browned. Add zucchini, yellow squash, green chile, and corn.

2. Stir and cook over low heat for 10 minutes, or until squash softens. Stir in cumin and oregano, add stock, and simmer for 10 more minutes. Season with salt and pepper and serve.

CHILES RELLENOS

For more than a century, Chope's Bar & Café, in La Mesa, has offered authentic traditional New Mexican food in the family's 150-year-old home. Located 20 miles south of Las Cruces and listed on the National Register of Historic Places, Chope's kitchen dishes out New Mexico home cooking that's as good as your abuela's, and that includes these famous chiles rellenos.

Makes 1 dozen

12 firm, long green chiles
1 pound yellow longhorn cheese
¾ cup flour
2 cups lard
4 eggs, separated

1. Roast and peel chile.
2. Cut the cheese into 12 strips, making each strip 3 to 4 inches long and ½-inch square in thickness. Near the top of each chile, make a slit on one side about an inch long and insert a cheese strip. Roll the chile in the flour until well coated and set aside.
3. In a deep skillet, melt the lard to medium hot. Keep stove set to medium.
4. Beat the egg whites until peaks form. Beat the egg yolks and fold into the whites. Dip the floured chile into the egg batter until well coated, then fry in lard until golden brown. (The egg will burn if the lard is too hot, so be careful.) Drain well and serve warm.

FRED HARVEY'S FAMOUS HOSPITALITY

Fred Harvey set out to "civilize" the West by revolutionizing how train passengers traveled. He built an empire of handsome hotels for weary travelers and restaurants serving fine fare. At its peak, the Fred Harvey Company operated 84 Harvey Houses from Chicago to Los Angeles, including the Castañeda Hotel, in Las Vegas, and La Fonda, in Santa Fe, both now lovingly renovated. Fred Harvey also ran 30 dining cars on the Santa Fe Railway—including the famous Turquoise Room, the private dining car of the Super Chief, the flagship of the Atchison, Topeka & Santa Fe Railway. Passengers craving fish could dine on fresh-caught New Mexico trout supplied by the Fred Harvey Creamery, in Las Vegas. The only requirement: You had to order that particular dinner from the chef on the Super Chief's first night out, so the trout could be picked up when the train stopped in Las Vegas.

HARVEY SMASH BURGER

"We put a lot of love into making the Harvey Smash Burger at Bar Castañeda," says acclaimed chef and New Mexico native Sean Sinclair, who owns the popular restaurant, housed in the Castañeda Hotel, a restored former Harvey House in Las Vegas, New Mexico. "It's one of the most memorable burgers you'll ever have. From sourcing beef for the patty to making the buns from scratch, a lot of steps make this simple dish special." Our March 2022 issue detailed its delectable parts; add a second patty for a heftier smash.

Serves 4

BURGERS

1½ **pounds ground beef, divided into**
   4 patties
½ **pound Tucumcari Mountain Cheese green**
   chile cheddar, grated
½ **cup New Mexico green chile, roasted,**
   peeled, seeded, and chopped
4 **of your favorite hamburger buns**
   or brioche-style hamburger buns
Sauce Castañeda (recipe follows)
2 **large dill pickles, sliced**
1 **small red onion, shaved**
1 **large tomato, sliced**
1 **cup shredded lettuce**

SAUCE CASTAÑEDA

Makes about 1½ cups

1 **cup mayonnaise (Sinclair uses Duke's Real**
   Mayonnaise)
1 **tablespoon Worcestershire sauce**
1 **medium dill pickle, minced**
½ **cup ketchup**
1 **tablespoon ground black pepper**
1 **tablespoon celery salt**

1. Portion beef into 4 balls and season each with salt and pepper, then smash them onto the griddle. The smashing creates a lot of surface area for the Maillard reaction, which makes the beef crispy, brown, and delicious.
2. Get a good sear on the first side. When you flip the burgers, top with some green chile and the cheese, then put a lid on the pan so the cheese melts. Sinclair cooks these burgers to medium well.
3. Mix Sauce Castañeda ingredients together in a bowl.
4. Toast and lightly steam buns, then sauce both sides generously. Sinclair likes his toppings on the bottom bun. Layer two or three pickle slices, red onion, tomato, and lettuce, then the chile-cheese-topped burger. (Add an extra patty for a hefty double chile cheeseburger.) Prepare to swoon after your first bite.

CHICKEN RANCHEROS WITH GREEN CHILE

Along the majestic High Road to Taos, Peñasco's Sugar Nymphs Bistro, housed in a whimsical building painted with colorful murals, has dazzled diners with made-from-scratch creative fare for more than two decades. The co-owners, chef Kai Harper Leah and pastry chef Ki Holste, created this versatile ranchero sauce for several purposes: to ladle over grilled chicken breasts with mashed potatoes and seasonal veggies, as a base for green chile alfredo pasta sauce, and as a topping for eggs at brunch. Try it with chicken for a flavorful dinner, then use the leftovers for Sunday brunch.

Makes enough sauce for 6 to 8 servings

1 cup diced yellow onion
4 cloves diced garlic
½ teaspoon salt
½ teaspoon cumin
1 to 2 teaspoons Chimayó
   red chile
½ teaspoon smoked paprika
½ cup green chile, chopped
½ chicken or vegetable bouillon
   cube
1 cup of water
½ cup canned fire-roasted
   tomatoes (or you can roast
   them yourself)
1 to 2 tablespoons cornstarch
   whisked with 2 tablespoons
   water
6 to 8 chicken breasts, grilled
Mashed potatoes for 6 to 8
   servings

1. Sauté onion and garlic until the onion is translucent.
2. Stir in salt, cumin, red chile, and smoked paprika. Then add green chile, bouillon cube, water, and tomatoes.
3. Stir in cornstarch slurry to thicken the sauce. Let the sauce simmer for about 20 minutes. It is ready to serve with chicken and potatoes once you've tasted it and adjusted the seasonings to your liking.

CHERRY PASTELITOS
(WITH) BIZCOCHITOS CRUST

This Chef Johnny Vee recipe from our June 2021 issue makes a sweet fruit-filled handpie, or empanada, wrapped in the anise-flavored crust of New Mexico's state cookie. Many New Mexicans make a simpler version by dividing the dough in half and rolling each half into ⅛-inch-thick sheets. With this method, you'd spread filling on the bottom sheet and place the second sheet on top. Gently press the edges together, brush with egg wash, sprinkle with cinnamon sugar, and bake as directed below. Allow to cool before cutting into squares.

Serves 12

PASTRY

1½ cups plus 3 tablespoons all-purpose flour
¾ teaspoon salt
¼ teaspoon cinnamon
1 teaspoon aniseed
¾ cup unsalted butter (1½ sticks), cold
6 tablespoons ice water (approximately)
1½ tablespoons brandy

1. Combine flour, salt, cinnamon, and aniseed in a large bowl.
2. Using a cheese grater, grate the butter over the flour mixture. With your hands, work butter into flour until dough is in pea-size pieces.
3. Add water and brandy and mix dough until it sticks together, being careful not to break butter into smaller pieces while blending in the water. (Add water slowly; you may not need it all.)
4. Turn onto lightly floured board and knead until dough just comes together. Wrap in plastic wrap, flatten into a disk, and refrigerate for 30 minutes, or until firm and ready to roll.

FILLING

3 cups fresh or frozen cherries, pitted
½ cup brown sugar
1¾ teaspoon ground cinnamon, divided
⅛ teaspoon ground nutmeg
½ teaspoon almond extract
1 large egg, beaten with 1 tablespoon cold water
1 tablespoon sugar
Powdered sugar for dusting

1. Preheat the oven to 375°. Line a baking sheet with parchment paper.
2. In a medium saucepan, stir together the cherries, brown sugar, ¾ teaspoon cinnamon, nutmeg, and almond extract

and bring to a boil. Turn to medium low and simmer for 10 minutes. Remove from heat and allow to cool.

3. Roll the dough out to ⅛-inch thick and cut circles with a 4-inch cookie cutter or glass, making each cut as close as possible to the next. (Scraps may be re-rolled and cut.)

4. Working with one piece of dough at a time and using a pastry brush, brush a ¼-inch border of egg wash around the perimeter of the dough. Spoon 2 tablespoons of cherries (about 6 halves)—leaving behind most of the juice—on one half of each circle, then fold it over into a half-moon. Do not overfill. Crimp the edges tightly with a fork dipped in flour to seal. Juice may be reserved as a sauce. Repeat the process until all of the dough has been used.

5. Mix remaining teaspoon of cinnamon with sugar in a small bowl. Brush each pastry lightly with remaining egg wash and sprinkle lightly with cinnamon sugar.

6. Bake for about 20 minutes, until lightly browned. Allow to cool before removing them from the baking sheet. Garnish with light dusting of powdered sugar.

CHOKECHERRY JELLY

The chokecherry, a native shrub or small tree, thrives in New Mexico. In mid-August it produces a wild black cherry with a sour taste that sweetens when dried or cooked. The juice, loaded with antioxidants, makes a wonderful jelly. Eloise Henry, of Ratón, shared her Certo gelatin recipe in *New Mexico's Tasty Traditions*, by Sharon Niederman, a cookbook published by *New Mexico Magazine* in 2010.

Makes 6 jars

3 cups prepared chokecherry juice
6½ cups sugar
2 packets (6 ounces) Certo gelatin

1. In a heavy-bottomed pan, combine the juice and the sugar. Mix well. Stir constantly on high heat. Bring to a full rolling boil that continues while you stir. Add the Certo all at once while you keep stirring. Bring to a full rolling boil again and allow to boil for 1 minute. Remove from heat. Skim off the foam.
2. Pour the hot liquid through a funnel into sterilized jars placed on a tray. Seal and store in refrigerator.

THE SWEETEST CHERRIES

If life is a bowl of cherries, then a good life awaits you in New Mexico, where you can fill your bowl to brimming with fresh cherries grown throughout the state. The season starts in June in New Mexico's cooler regions, and lasts three to four weeks. That's when you'll find fans of this sweet stone fruit climbing ladders in backyards and in orchards, cherry-picking their favorites. Sweet varieties include Rainier and Bing, while Montmorency and Danube are among the sour offerings. These red gems, plentiful today, were first brought to New Mexico by Spanish settlers, who introduced an array of fruit—apricots, pears, apples, plums, and quinces—as well as other foods. According to historical records, cherries were growing in New Mexico as early as 1630.

GREEN CHILE MILKSHAKE

This delectable recipe for a New Mexican twist on an all-American classic has appeared in several of our cookbooks and in our September 2016 issue. It comes courtesy of Josie and Teako Nunn, owners of Sparky's Burgers, BBQ & Espresso, in Hatch. If you're in the neighborhood, you can't miss this longtime green chile cheeseburger hub, complete with giant statues of Colonel Sanders, the A&W Root Beer family, and a robot alien. There's no better spot to slurp a chile shake.

Serves 1 to 2

20 ounces soft-serve vanilla ice cream (or substitute regular ice cream, slightly softened)

¼ cup New Mexico Hatch green chile, roasted, peeled, seeded, and chopped

1. Whip ingredients in a blender.
2. Pour into glass and enjoy.

DON SILVIARES, EL VERDULERO

BY LEVI ROMERO

On a warm fall afternoon, I accompany my cousin to the barbershop. It is late in the day, and the last of the barber's clients trickle out as we walk in. The early autumn glow of the elm trees' golden hues shimmers beyond the shop windows. →

My primo introduces me to the barber. "So you're from Embudo?" the barber asks me, the snip of his scissors rhythmically slicing through the slow afternoon. "When I was a kid growing up in Dawson, there was a man that went every year from Embudo to sell his chile, apples, flour, and other products. It was an annual ritual, and in the fall, everyone in the village would be anticipating his arrival on his horse-drawn wagon." My primo and I listen intently.

The barber's story wonderfully articulates the relationship between one man selling his produce and the community to which he traveled, almost a hundred miles annually, to deliver products that would sustain the village for another year.

But the barber's story has a personal relevance more important to me than the concept of bartering traditions. Could the man on the wagon have been my grandfather, who operated a vegetable trade route from Embudo to Cimarrón in the thirties, forties, and early fifties? The barber continues, "The entire village would be waiting for the day when we would see him coming down the road."

My primo's eyes gaze at me from under his crinkled forehead, his head held steady by the barber's hand. "Every fall, upon his return, the kids from the village would run down the road to greet him. Some would jump onto his wagon and ride with him into the village as he laughed and played his harmonica. The other kids would run ahead,

> "WHEN I WAS A KID GROWING UP IN DAWSON, THERE WAS A MAN THAT WENT EVERY YEAR FROM EMBUDO TO SELL HIS CHILE, APPLES, FLOUR, AND OTHER PRODUCTS. IT WAS AN ANNUAL RITUAL, AND IN THE FALL, EVERYONE IN THE VILLAGE WOULD BE ANTICIPATING HIS ARRIVAL ON HIS HORSE-DRAWN WAGON," SAYS THE BARBER.

announcing his arrival: '¡Aquí viene Don Silviares, aquí viene Don Silviares!' "

"Don Silviares, that was his name—Don Silviares!" exclaims the barber. "Don Silviares's wagon was filled with bushels of fruit and sacks of flour, chile verde, ristras, manzanas, peras, melones, ciruelas, sandías. ¡Eee, quien sabe que tanto que más!"

As I listen to his story, I can see the cornucopia of bushels filled with apples, pears, melons, and plums, the sacks of green chile, red chile ristras, watermelons, and who knows what else! I imagine the sound of my grandfather's prized stallion, El Elefante, pulling the wagonload of produce, his sweaty flanks and large hoofs kicking up dust. I hear the clinking and clanking of bridle, harness, and leather in rhythm with my grandfather's song.

A few years later, at Doña Petra Sanchez's 80th birthday celebration, Mrs. Sanchez introduces me to her sister and a childhood friend. After the cordial introductions, I ask them where they are from. "We're from Dawson," says Mrs. Sanchez's younger sister. "Oh, I've heard the name before, but I can't recall where Dawson is. Where is it?" I ask.

"You mean, where was it?" she says. "It's not there any longer," adds her friend. "Dawson was over by Ratón, but no one lives there anymore. It's an abandoned mining town." "Near Ratón?" I ask. "Yes," she replies. "My grandfather used to sell and barter fruit and vegetables out that way," I tell her. "Who was your grandfather?" →

"His name was Silviares Duran. I've been told that the people from Cimarrón and around that area knew him as Don Silviares."

"Don Silviares?" She ponders the name. "I remember him," she says, as if a long-distant memory has entered her recollections. "You do?" I ask enthusiastically. "Yes, yes." She turns to her friend and asks her, "¿Te acuerdas de Don Silviares, aquel hombre que venía todos los años del Embudo a vender fruta?" "Si, me acuerdo bien," she says. "En mamá le llamava El Verdulero."

A verdulero is a vegetable grower. They reminisce about Don Silviares, my grandfather, who they recalled being their family's favorite fruit grower. My tío Celestino remembered accompanying my grandfather on some of his trips to Dawson. He said that my grandfather and his vegetables were so highly regarded that when a kid from the household would announce that there was someone outside selling fruit and vegetables, they could hear the woman of the house say, "Si es El Verdulero, sí, queremos." The quality of my grandfather's produce guaranteed that his harvest had a market

> HE SAID THAT MY GRANDFATHER AND HIS VEGETABLES WERE SO HIGHLY REGARDED THAT WHEN A KID FROM THE HOUSEHOLD WOULD ANNOUNCE THAT THERE WAS SOMEONE OUTSIDE SELLING FRUIT AND VEGETABLES, THEY COULD HEAR THE WOMAN OF THE HOUSE SAY, "SI ES EL VERDULERO, SÍ, QUEREMOS."

of customers who preferred his fare over someone else's. I also later learn that Dolores Huerta, the labor leader and co-founder with César Chávez of the United Farm Workers, was born in Dawson.

For many nuevomexicanos, harvest season stirs up stories of family traditions associated with the unmistakable scent of chile roasting and a yearning for locally produced vegetables. Green and red chile sauces, chicos, posole, atole, pastelitos, home-canned fruits and vegetables, and other treasured family foods and recipes enter people's memories and conversations. Unlike back when fruit growers like Don Silviares traveled long distances to deliver their produce, these days we visit farmers' markets, the grocery store, or our favorite grower's stand to purchase fruits and vegetables. If we are fortunate, relationships are formed with these providers. We carry on in the manner of our antepasados, celebrating life with homegrown foods and healthy eating, while forming lifelong friendships with the verduleros who provide our tables with the nurturing sustenance to carry us through the rest of the year. 🥄

LEVI ROMERO *was selected as the inaugural New Mexico poet laureate in 2020. He is the author of several poetry collections and anthologies and is an associate professor in the Chicana and Chicano Studies department at the University of New Mexico. Romero is from the Embudo Valley of northern New Mexico.*

SAVORY PUMPKIN (AND) APPLE GRIDDLE CAKES (WITH) CHUTNEY (AND) CRÈME FRAÎCHE

Pumpkins played a prominent role in early Native cuisine. A member of the squash family, pumpkins are one of the Three Sisters—corn, beans, and squash. When planted together, each helps the others to flourish and grow. Pumpkins were part of the Indigenous diet well before Spanish settlers made their way to New Mexico, providing blossoms for stews, seeds for snacking, and other culinary contributions. In Taos, chefs Wilks and Colleen Medley use local pumpkins at their eclectic restaurant, Medley, in dishes such as pumpkin bisque and pumpkin lava cake. Wilks shared this recipe for a fall breakfast feast featuring pumpkin, apples, and other seasonal ingredients in our October 2022 issue.

Serves 6

GRIDDLE CAKES

2 cups all-purpose flour
½ cup sugar
1 teaspoon baking powder
1 teaspoon kosher salt
1 teaspoon ground cinnamon
¼ teaspoon ground clove
¼ teaspoon ground allspice
¼ teaspoon ground ginger
¼ teaspoon ground nutmeg
3 eggs
1 cup heavy cream
15 ounces pumpkin puree
1 cup grated Honeycrisp apple
3 tablespoons melted butter, plus more
    for cooking

1. In a medium mixing bowl, whisk together the flour, sugar, baking powder, salt, and spices until well combined.
2. In another medium mixing bowl, combine the eggs, cream, pumpkin puree, and grated apple.
3. Slowly add the dry ingredients to the wet ones, whisking continuously until batter is smooth. Stir in the melted butter and mix well.
4. Heat a large sauté pan or griddle over medium heat and lightly butter. Ladle about ¼ cup of batter into the pan to form each cake. Cook for about 2 to 3 minutes on each side, then set aside and keep warm. Continue until all the batter has been cooked.

SPICED APPLE AND GOLDEN RAISIN CHUTNEY

2 tablespoons butter
2 cups peeled and diced Honeycrisp apple
1 cup golden raisins
1 cup diced red bell pepper
½ cup brown sugar
1 cup dry white wine
2 tablespoons whole-grain mustard
½ teaspoon prepared horseradish
¼ teaspoon smoked paprika
1 teaspoon salt, or to taste

1. Melt the butter in a medium-size saucepan; add the apple, raisins, and bell pepper. Cook over medium heat until softened, about 5 to 7 minutes.
2. Stir in the brown sugar, wine, mustard, horseradish, smoked paprika, and salt.
3. Bring to a simmer and cook over medium-low heat for about 20 minutes, until the liquid has cooked down and become very syrupy.

CARAWAY CRÈME FRAÎCHE

½ teaspoon caraway seeds
1 cup crème fraîche
Pinch of kosher salt

1. Toast caraway seeds on a cookie sheet in a 350° preheated oven for about 3 minutes, until fragrant.
2. Transfer the seeds to a spice blender and pulse until very fine.
3. In a medium mixing bowl, whisk together the crème fraîche, caraway seeds, and salt. Refrigerate until serving.

ASSEMBLY

1. Lay three griddle cakes on each plate, overlapping them slightly.
2. Top each cake with 1 tablespoon of chutney. (Reserve remaining chutney in refrigerator for up to 2 weeks.)
3. Finish with a liberal drizzle of the caraway crème fraîche.

BISON CHILE BEANS

James Beard Award–winning cookbook author and Native foods historian and educator Lois Ellen Frank shares one of her favorite recipes for using dried foods from the previous growing season. She cooks the stew in a large cast-iron pot that was passed down to her by her mother. "The taste from the cast iron makes this chile bean stew even more delicious," she says. "It can be made with meat or just with beans and vegetables and tastes great either way. It makes a hearty meal by itself or a side to any feast. It is a favorite at all family and ceremonial gatherings."

Serves 8 to 12

4 to 6 cloves garlic
2 teaspoons sunflower oil
1 pound ground bison
1 large yellow onion, chopped (approximately 2 cups)
1 green bell pepper, seeded and chopped
1 28-ounce can whole peeled tomatoes with basil
2½ cups cooked dark red kidney beans
2½ cups cooked pinto beans
2 cups cooked corn kernels (fresh, frozen, or canned)
3 tablespoons dried mild New Mexico red chile powder
1 teaspoon kosher salt (or to taste)
¼ teaspoon dried thyme (or to taste)
½ teaspoon dried Mexican oregano (or to taste)
4 cups water or bean juice

1. Heat a small dry, seasoned sauté pan until it is hot. Place the raw peeled garlic in the pan and cook, stirring occasionally until the garlic begins to brown on all sides. Cook for approximately 6 minutes, depending on your flame. Stir to make sure that it evenly browns on all sides, but it should not be completely brown. You should still have some parts that retain their original color. Remove from heat. Allow to cool and then finely chop it.

2. Heat the oil in a cast-iron pot or soup pot over medium-high heat until hot but not smoking. Add the meat and brown for several minutes. Add the onions and sauté for 4 minutes, until translucent, stirring to prevent burning. Add bell peppers and sauté another 2 minutes. Add the garlic, stir, and cook for an additional minute.

3. Cut each of the whole tomatoes from the can into 8 pieces (a large dice) and add them to the pan. Cook for another 2 minutes, stirring constantly. Add the kidney beans and pinto beans and stir well. Stir in the corn kernels and cook for an additional 2 minutes to blend all the ingredients. Stir in the red chile powder, salt, thyme, and oregano. Add the water and bring to a boil. Reduce the heat and let simmer for 20 minutes, stirring occasionally to prevent burning. Serve hot with warm bread or homemade corn or flour tortillas.

Note: Frank recommends cooking the beans in a slow cooker overnight, adding additional water so that you can use the liquid (bean juice) in soups and stews.

STUFFED ACORN SQUASH

Chef Travis Tegreeney, a Laguna Pueblo member who was then the chef at Acoma Pueblo's Y'aak'a Café, shared this recipe in a November 2016 *New Mexico Magazine* article about the prized New Mexico piñon nut. Cooking with piñon is "part of our culture, and you can use it in many ways," he says. "When I was young, the hunters would use it in deer stew with pumpkin, hominy, and sweet corn." Here, piñons lend a sweet, buttery flavor to roasted acorn squash, creating a savory side dish.

Serves 4

2 acorn squash
Olive oil
Salt, pepper, and ground
    coriander to taste
3 cups chicken stock
1½ cups wild rice
½ cup piñon nuts

1. Halve the acorn squash lengthwise and scoop out seeds. Brush the flesh with olive oil and sprinkle lightly with salt, pepper, and coriander.
2. Place in 350° oven for 35 to 40 minutes, until fork tender.
3. Meanwhile, bring the chicken stock to a rolling boil, add the wild rice, and season with salt and pepper. When the mixture returns to a boil, reduce heat, cover, and simmer for 40 minutes, until tender.
4. Heat a sauté pan on medium, add piñon nuts, and cook for 3 to 4 minutes, stirring occasionally to avoid burning. Remove from heat when the nuts are lightly toasted. Add to wild rice.
5. Stuff rice mixture into cooked squash and serve. Top with your favorite chile sauce if desired.

GREEN CHILE STEW

Hatch Chile Express not only grows great chile in New Mexico's most famous growing region; it's also run by a third-generation farmer who happens to be the son of Jim Lytle, the namesake of Big Jim, a prized variety of New Mexico chile. So you know this green chile stew recipe from our October 2021 issue is the real deal. Dress it up with bowls of grated cheese, chopped green onions, lime wedges, and tortillas or cornbread.

Serves 4

1 tablespoon vegetable oil
½ pound round steak, cubed
½ pound lean pork, cubed
1 medium onion, chopped
5 medium potatoes, cubed
1 pound Hatch green chile,
   roasted, peeled, seeded,
   and chopped
1 teaspoon garlic salt
½ teaspoon pepper
½ teaspoon cumin
1 pinch oregano

1. In a large saucepan, warm vegetable oil over medium heat. Add beef, pork, and onion. Sauté until meat has browned and onion is tender.
2. Add 4 cups water and the potatoes. Cook over medium heat, stirring occasionally, for 25 minutes, or until potatoes are tender.
3. Add remaining ingredients. Reduce heat and simmer 15 minutes. Adjust salt to taste and serve.

NEW MEXICO'S CHILE OBSESSION

New Mexico is world-famous for its chile, and rightly so. Reams have been written about the prized green chile grown in Hatch, in the southern part of the state, and the revered red chile from Chimayó, in the north. John Crenshaw described the allure in his essay "Chile—New Mexico's Fiery Soul," first published in the magazine's *The Best from New Mexico Kitchens* cookbook in 1978:

"Capsaicin, or an isomer thereof, is that oily, orangish acid layered along the seeds and veins of the chile pod ... Capsaicin, then, makes chile chile, gives it the piquancy ranging from innocuous to incendiary, brings tears to the eater's eyes, blisters to his lips, fire to his belly—and joy to his heart.

"Chile: Spicy, flavorful, unique—indeed a symbol specific to the heart of the Southwest and a fitting catalyst for that ancient disease of the displaced.

"Chile: Ancient, honored, symbolic. A spice—and a fruit unto itself." ▓

GREEN CHILE MAC AND CHEESE

Walk into the Buckhorn Saloon & Opera House, in Pinos Altos, north of Silver City, and you're whisked back some 150 years to the heyday of this Old West mining town. The Buckhorn, built in the style of the watering holes once frequented by miners, is known for its steaks and seafood. Owner and chef Thomas Bock pays tribute to New Mexico's most famous crop with this signature twist on a classic American comfort food. The old-time miners would have loved it.

Serves 4 to 6

1 pound penne pasta
8 tablespoons (1 stick) butter
1¾ cup all-purpose flour
1 cup whole milk
2 pounds Hatch green chile, roasted and chopped
3½ ounces chicken base
4 cups Jack cheese, plus 1 extra cup for topping
1 cup cilantro
2 cups panko bread crumbs

1. Preheat oven to 350°. Bring a large pot of salted water to a boil. (It should taste like the sea.)
2. Add the pasta and cook until al dente. Drain the pasta and put it back in the pot.
3. Meanwhile, melt the butter and, over medium heat, whisk with the flour to make a roux. Add the milk, green chile, and chicken base while stirring. The mixture should be creamy, not gummy.
4. Add this mixture to the pasta and fold in the cheese. Add the cilantro and portion out into ramekins for individual servings.
5. Top filled ramekins with panko and more cheese. Bake until bubbly and dark blond on top.

ROLLED GREEN CHILE CHEESE ENCHILADAS

Chef and author Cheryl Alters Jamison was a teenager in Galesburg, Illinois, when she came across a green chile enchilada casserole recipe in her father's copy of *The Republican Congressional Cook Book*. It was contributed by New Mexico congressman Manuel Luján Jr. The dish intrigued her and ultimately helped shape her destiny: She later moved to New Mexico and started writing cookbooks with her late husband, Bill Jamison. Together they earned four James Beard Awards. "Over the years, my enchilada recipe has evolved to this one," she says in a feature from December 2013. "Freshly poached chicken makes an especially appealing filling, but you can also use about 3 cups of shredded roast chicken or other cooked chicken. The filling mixture can be prepared a day ahead of when you plan to assemble the enchiladas."

Serves 6

3 chicken breasts, bone in, skin on;
    or 2 breasts and 2 thighs
3 cups chicken stock
½ cup chopped onion
3 garlic cloves, minced
¼ teaspoon salt
Vegetable oil for frying
12 corn tortillas (see page 12)
3 cups green chile sauce (see page 9)
½ cup onion, minced
8 ounces cream cheese, softened
8 ounces (2 cups) shredded Monterey Jack
    or mild cheddar cheese, or a combination

FILLING

1. In a large saucepan, combine stock with chicken, garlic, and salt and bring just to a boil. Reduce heat to a low simmer and poach chicken until cooked through and very tender (25 to 30 minutes). Let chicken cool a few minutes in the liquid. Drain chicken and, when cool enough to handle, shred into bite-size pieces. (Save cooking liquid for soups or sauces.)

ASSEMBLY

1. Preheat oven to 350°. Grease a large baking dish. Spread a thin layer (about ¼ cup) of chile sauce in baking dish. In small skillet, heat ½ to 1 inch of oil until it ripples. With tongs, dunk each tortilla in oil long enough for it to go limp (a matter of seconds). Blot with paper towels if you wish.
2. Dip tortilla in chile sauce. Top with about ¼ cup of chicken, a couple of teaspoons of minced onion, 1½ tablespoons of cream cheese, and a heaping tablespoon of shredded cheese. Roll up tortilla snugly but not tightly. Transfer enchilada to baking dish. Repeat with the rest of the tortillas and filling.

Top enchiladas with any remaining minced onion and pour the remaining sauce evenly over them. Scatter rest of cheese over the top.

3. Bake about 20 minutes, until enchiladas are heated through and sauce and cheese are bubbly. Serve immediately.

RED CHILE PORK ROAST
WITH LINCOLN COUNTY PUDDING

This easy recipe for a red-chile-rubbed roast comes from Adela Amador, longtime food columnist for *New Mexico Magazine* and author of *Southwest Flavor: Adela Amador's Tales from the Kitchen—Recipes and Stories from New Mexico Magazine*, published in 2000. The accompanying recipe for Lincoln County Pudding is from *The Best from New Mexico Kitchens*, with this note: "When in New Mexico ... some British immigrants looked at their Yorkshire pudding recipes, looked at the materials on hand, and came up with this zingy version of an old favorite."

Serves 8 to 10

RED CHILE PORK ROAST

2 teaspoons garlic salt
1 teaspoon pepper
2 teaspoons ground red chile
1 boneless rolled pork loin roast (4 to 4½ pounds)
1 or 2 medium onions, sliced
1 cup water

1. Preheat oven to 325°. Combine garlic salt, pepper, and red chile powder; rub over entire roast.
2. Place roast with fat side up on greased rack in a roasting pan. Top with onion. Pour water into pan. Bake, uncovered, for 2 to 2½ hours. Let stand for 10 to 15 minutes before slicing.

LINCOLN COUNTY PUDDING

Pan drippings from roasted meat
¾ cup flour
½ teaspoon salt
2 tablespoons red chile powder
¼ teaspoon ground cumin
3 eggs
1 cup milk
1 tablespoon minced onion

1. Set the finished roast aside in a warm place. Turn the oven up to 450°.
2. Leave about ½ cup of drippings in the baking pan.
3. Mix flour, salt, chile powder, and cumin together.
4. Beat eggs, milk, and onion together, then beat in flour mixture. Turn into the hot drippings and bake for about 30 minutes. The pudding should puff and brown.
5. Cut into squares and serve right away with your roast.

NEW MEXICO APPLE PIE
WITH GREEN CHILE AND PIÑON

This bliss-inducing pie is made with ingredients grown in New Mexico—earthy green chile, sweet, buttery piñons, and fresh apples. It's the most frequently requested recipe from Kathy Knapp, former proprietor of the Pie-O-Neer café, who long reigned as the Pie Lady of Pie Town. She shared this recipe in our November 2022 issue. The celebrated bakery lives on, and the new owner continues to serve this signature pie.

2 unbaked pastry crusts (recipe follows)

5 to 6 large apples, peeled, cored, and sliced (Knapp uses half Granny Smith and half Fuji or Gala; any apple will work except Red Delicious)

1 tablespoon lemon juice

½ cup sugar (more if using only tart apples)

2 teaspoons cinnamon

2 to 3 tablespoons cornstarch or flour

½ to 1 cup green chile, roasted, peeled, seeded, and chopped, drained if using frozen (medium heat preferred)

¾ cup piñon (pine) nuts, toasted

1 to 2 tablespoons butter, cubed

1 egg white mixed with 3 tablespoons water for egg wash (optional)

1 to 2 teaspoons decorating sugar or table sugar for sprinkling on top (optional)

1. Preheat oven to 425°. Combine apples, lemon juice, sugar, and cinnamon in a bowl. Let sit a few minutes so the apples can macerate. Add cornstarch or flour and gently mix to dissolve. Add chile and mix gently to incorporate. If chile is very wet, more cornstarch or flour may be added.

2. Place bottom pastry in pie pan (Pyrex or suitable glass preferred). Scatter toasted and cooled piñon nuts in bottom. Add apple mixture, mounding slightly in center, then dot with butter.

3. Use egg wash to coat rim of crust to create a seal. Place top crust on apples and crimp pastry edges together. Cut several steam holes, then brush with egg wash and sprinkle with decorating sugar or regular table sugar. (Egg wash and decorative sugar are optional but will result in a more polished-looking pie.) Decorate top crust with a pastry scrap cut to look like a chile and sprinkled with cinnamon.

4. Place pie in center of oven and bake for 15 to 20 minutes at 425°. Turn heat down to 350° and continue baking another 40 to 50 minutes, or until crust is golden brown and juices are bubbling from steam vents. If using glass pie pan, look at bottom of pie to ensure it is brown. If not, continue baking for another few minutes. If edges of crust begin to get too dark, cover with strips of aluminum foil or use pie-crust shields.

5. Cool on wire rack for one hour. Enjoy with ice cream.

PIE CRUST

(from Adela Amador's Southwest Flavor)

Makes an 8- or 9-inch two-crust pie

2 cups flour
1 teaspoon salt
16 tablespoons (2 sticks) butter
5 tablespoons ice water (spooned from cup
with ice cubes floating in water)

1. Mix all ingredients except water, then sprinkle water in a tablespoon at a time, until flour is completely moistened and dough holds together.
2. For easy handling of dough, cut in half and place between two pieces of wax paper. Roll flat. You are now ready to follow any pie recipe you'd like.

THE STORY OF PIE TOWN

Along US 60, where the road crosses the Continental Divide, lies a 20th-century homesteading community, an old stopping place for cattle-driving cowboys and for travelers who braked for homemade apple pies. Clyde Norman started selling his pies at Norman's Place in the 1920s, and the community soon became known as Pie Town. When a drought in the 1950s forced many to leave Pie Town, the pies disappeared. That is, until 1995, when Kathy Knapp and her mother, Mary Knapp, drove through Pie Town and discovered the old Thunderbird Trading Post was for sale. They bought the structure, which dates to 1945, and opened it as the Pie-O-Neer, bringing pie back to Pie Town. After a long and storied run that put the town in the international spotlight, Kathy retired and sold her bakery to new owners, who keep the legacy flourishing.

PIÑON COOKIES

New Mexico piñons have been prized for centuries by Indigenous people who ate them for snacks, then by Spanish settlers who added the tasty nuts to the traditional recipes they brought with them. This easy recipe yields delectable results.

Makes 5 dozen cookies

4 eggs
1½ cups granulated sugar
½ teaspoon grated lemon rind
1½ cups sifted flour
½ teaspoon salt
¼ cup confectioners' sugar
1 cup piñon nuts

1. Preheat oven to 350°. Grease and flour cookie sheets.
2. Put eggs and granulated sugar in the top of a double boiler over hot water. Beat with a rotary or electric beater until mixture is lukewarm. Remove from water and beat until foaming and cool. Add lemon rind and fold in flour and salt. Drop by teaspoonfuls onto cookie sheets. Sprinkle with confectioners' sugar and nuts. Let stand for 10 minutes.
3. Bake for about 10 minutes. Let cool and remove from cookie sheets.

APPLE COCKTAIL

Created by Arturo Jaramillo, owner of the James Beard America's Classics Award–winning restaurant Rancho de Chimayó, this thoroughly New Mexican cocktail makes good use of the village of Chimayó's apples and cider.

Serves 1

1½ ounces tequila
1 ounce homemade New Mexico
    sweet apple cider
¼ ounce lemon juice
¼ ounce crème de cassis
Apple wedge for garnish

1. Shake ingredients together, chill, and serve with a wedge of New Mexico-grown apple over the rim of the glass.

THE ESSENCE OF CHRISTMAS

BY INEZ RUSSELL GOMEZ

The essence of Christmas can be served in one bowl. The bowl is small and white. It holds freshly made red chile, the "fancy kind." That means instead of using chile powder or store-bought frozen, my mom took the dried pods, blended them with hot water, and mixed the liquid with shredded pork, salt, and garlic, using the pork juices to flavor the chile in a combination that creates one of the best tastes on earth.

It is the perfect Christmas meal, one my mother prepared every Christmas Eve—even the one we almost spent apart. Like those in many families, the customs of my youth transformed as I grew, married, and began my own family. The tradition of my adult years over two decades of married life was to head to Taos Pueblo for Christmas Eve. →

My husband, son, and I, along with his many relatives at the pueblo, came to watch bonfire flames lick the sky as people carried a statue of the Virgin Mary through the village in procession.

One year, though, I was torn. My mother was frail and growing more so. Either I would spend Christmas Eve with her in Santa Fe—without my son and husband—or I had to leave her alone. She told me to go.

I stayed. It turned out to be our last Christmas together.

We went to early Mass. Then it was back to Mom's house, where the chile simmered on the stove, a big pot for just two people. On a plate nearby were stacks of empanaditas that she and I had made, our Christmas specialty ready for whoever might stop by over the holidays.

All the elements of my childhood celebrations came together.

There was the traditional food, chile and empanaditas, the sweet meat turnovers that can make a meal by themselves. When I was a child in Las Vegas, New Mexico, we expected the arrival of dozens of cousins, many aunts and uncles, and friends from town.

Then, the offerings were more varied than our simple bowl of red chile. Posole on Christmas Eve, with red chile nearby to add color and flavor; fresh tamales, usually from my Auntie Rita. The sisters split the Christmas work. My mom made the empanaditas and, when needed, sopaipillas, while my aunt did tamales. Each family added their own chile, posole, or enchiladas. The idea was to have enough food so that anyone who stopped in could be fed.

My grandma Celia was the bizcochito maker, turning out dozens of the sugar-cinnamon-anise cookies, so light and delicate they dissolved on the first bite. I can see her hands rolling out the dough, using a small shot glass to cut the cookies, then fluting the edges by hand.

My job was to dip the cookies into a sugar-and-cinnamon mix, which I did while standing on a small stool over the kitchen table as my grandma shaped the cookies.

Family was blended into those foods of Christmas. Not only the immediate relatives—the ones who came and ate, dropping off their own baked goods or small presents—but the ones who had lived before, who had taught my grandma, mother, and aunts to cook these foods, especially the complex empanaditas.

Making empanaditas is not a task for the meek. The process is laborious, with the cook first preparing the roasts—pork and beef—and adding the spices, nuts, and raisins. My mother cooked the meat first. Then came the shredding of the roasts through a metal grinder, my brother and me relishing how big chunks went in and small pieces emerged. Then my mom would add the other ingredients and leave them simmering overnight.

The flavors merged by morning, and then Momma would begin the process of folding the dough around the meat. She'd plop a big spoon of filling in the middle of the dough, bring the edges together, and close and twist them into a seal. Then, with hot oil bubbling at the perfect temperature, we fried the empanaditas, watching so that the dough turned a perfect golden color.

Red chile and empanaditas. Family stopping by. Memories of holidays steeped in New Mexico hold fast to the heart. ♣

INEZ RUSSELL GOMEZ *is editorial page editor for the* Santa Fe New Mexican. *She grew up in Las Vegas, New Mexico, where her mother ran a small restaurant and her grandmother was renowned for her tortillas, sold at the Columbia Super Market. A version of this essay appeared in our December 2020 issue.*

KICKED-UP ATOLE

"A simple dish like atole puts one in touch with the New Mexican reality of earth and sky and growth and rain. That's why it is often called 'the breakfast of champions,'" wrote the beloved New Mexico author Rudolfo Anaya. Davida Becenti (Diné), executive chef of the Indian Pueblo Kitchen, in Albuquerque, shared this hearty, healthy recipe, a satisfying staple at this acclaimed restaurant focused on Indigenous cuisine. Becenti's instructions make for a thick, oatmeal-like texture; for more of an elixir, add water.

Serves 4

2 cups water
2 cups blue cornmeal
Pinch of salt
1 ounce (2 tablespoons) butter
½ cup brown sugar
Quinoa, amaranth, piñon, dried currants, sunflower and pumpkin seeds, strawberries, blueberries, and blackberries for garnish

1. Place the water in a small pot and bring to a boil. Slowly add the blue cornmeal and mix until smooth. Slowly add the salt, butter, and brown sugar while continuing to stir. Remove from heat and let set for 10 minutes before serving.

2. Garnish with grains, nuts, currants, seeds, and berries and serve with a slice of toasted, buttered Pueblo bread, traditionally baked in an horno, or hot buttered tortillas.

POSOLE

The Shed opened in 1953 and continues to thrive in a 17th-century hacienda in the heart of historic downtown Santa Fe. The family-run restaurant received a James Beard America's Classics Award for its "timeless appeal" and is revered for its traditional New Mexico cuisine. This recipe originally appeared in 1978's *The Best from New Mexico Kitchens.* The dish has long been part of Pueblo feast days as well as Christmas Eve, Christmas, and New Year's dinners.

Serves 16

1 pound lean pork shoulder
2 pounds frozen posole (hominy)
Juice of one lime
2 tablespoons coarse red chile
    powder
3 cloves garlic
¼ teaspoon dried oregano
3 tablespoons salt

1. Cook the pork in a pressure cooker, with water to cover, for 20 minutes. Reduce pressure under cold water. Open pot and add posole, lime juice, and red chile. Add water—about twice as much as the amount of posole. Cook for 45 minutes under pressure. Reduce pressure under cold water.

2. Remove the pork and cut up. Put posole, pork, garlic, oregano, and salt in a large, heavy covered pot and simmer 1 to 3 hours, or until hominy kernels have burst and are soft but not mushy. Serve alone or as a side dish. Freezes well.

Note: These times are set for Santa Fe's higher elevation. At lower elevations, where the boiling point is higher, you may wish to try shorter cooking times at first.

CARNE ADOVADA

This hearty New Mexico dish is a traditional favorite, served on its own, stuffed inside enchiladas or sopaipillas, or wrapped up in a burrito. It's a classic dish that originated more than a century ago as a way for pork to be preserved. This recipe comes from Atrisco Cafe & Bar, in Santa Fe. Atrisco owner George Gundrey's family history spans more than 75 years in the New Mexico restaurant business: His grandmother operated the now-shuttered Central Café in Albuquerque's Atrisco neighborhood; his aunt and uncle opened Tia Sophia's in Santa Fe; and his mother ran Tomasita's, with the help of famed chef Tomasita Leyba, for decades before Gundrey took over. The family's Albuquerque roots helped inspire Atrisco Cafe, which opened in 2009 and quickly became a locals' favorite.

Serves 4 to 6

Olive oil
2 pounds pork butt, cut into 1-inch cubes
20 ounces New Mexico red chile sauce (made with dried pods or red chile powder, or with frozen Bueno brand red chile puree)
1 tablespoon oregano
1 tablespoon cumin
1 tablespoon granulated garlic
1 tablespoon salt

1. Heat oil in a frying pan and sear pork, turning constantly. Cook until some pieces are seared brown.
2. Mix all other ingredients separately, adding water if necessary, so that mix is a little thicker than pasta sauce.
3. Combine seasoned chile mixture with seared pork cubes. Bake in oven at 350° until pork is nearly falling apart. Add more salt to taste if necessary.

A SEASONED BLEND

"New Mexico cuisine has come basically from the Native Americans, who first domesticated the essential plants. They are simple combinations of chile, beans, corn, squash, and meat. Years ago the meat was wild game, especially rabbit and deer. Chickens, sheep, and cattle came from Europe later. What we eat today is a woven blend of many cultures, prepared

with pride. They are a symbol of the past and the present, and provide a link in the chain of our Southwest heritage." 𝍫

—*Adela Amador,* from her introduction to *Southwest Flavor: Adela Amador's Tales from the*

GREEN CHILE CHICKEN POT PIE

This recipe from our January 2019 issue for what might just be the ultimate winter comfort food comes from former *New Mexico Magazine* senior editor Gwyneth Doland, who describes the dish as "enchilada casserole meets chicken soup for a real dose of love in a bowl." Because the recipe calls for many precooked ingredients, it's a great way to use up holiday leftovers, like roasted potatoes and peas. Feel free to make substitutions, such as turkey for chicken.

Serves 6

6 tablespoons (¾ stick) butter
1 cup diced onion
2 cloves garlic, minced
½ cup all-purpose flour
1 cup green chile, roasted, peeled, seeded, and diced
1½ cups milk
1 cup diced cooked potatoes
¾ cup diced cooked carrots or butternut squash
1 cup cooked or frozen corn kernels, green beans, or peas
2 cups cooked chicken, cubed
Salt and pepper to taste
2 chilled pie crusts (See page 85)
1 egg beaten with 1 tablespoon water

1. Preheat the oven to 375°. In a large saucepan over medium heat, melt the butter. Add the onion and garlic and sauté until translucent, about 10 to 15 minutes.

2. Reduce the heat to low. Add the flour, stirring well, and cook about 2 more minutes. Add the green chile and milk and cook until it starts to bubble and thicken. Remove the pot from the heat. Stir in the potatoes, vegetables, and chicken, then season to taste.

3. Roll out one pie crust and arrange it in the bottom of a deep-dish pie plate. Fill with the chicken mixture. Roll out the other crust, lay it over the top, and crimp to seal. Brush the crust with the egg wash and make 4 slits in the top to allow steam to escape. Put the pie plate on a baking sheet (to catch drips) and bake 45 minutes to 1 hour, until the crust is golden brown.

PUMPKIN, KALE, CORN, AND CHANTERELLE MUSHROOM ENCHILADAS WITH EAST INDIAN SPINACH PUREE AND SPICY GREEN RICE

Chef Joseph Wrede is celebrated for his creative combinations of flavors and textures, mixing local ingredients with global cuisines. He launched his culinary career in Taos in 1995 with the renowned Joseph's Table before relocating to Santa Fe and opening Joseph's Culinary Pub. This recipe reflects his playful approach, fusing a classic New Mexican dish with international influences. He recommends serving the ensemble with chopped radish and pico de gallo.

Serves 4

RED CHILE SAUCE

2 cups red chile pods
1 quart of water
1 tablespoon cooking oil
1 onion, diced
4 cloves garlic, minced
1 teaspoon oregano
1 teaspoon cumin
2 whole bay leaves

1. Remove chile tops and shake out seeds. Cover red chile pods with water. On high heat, bring chile to a boil in a medium pot. Boil for 10 minutes. Discard water. Place chile pods in a blender and let cool.
2. Over medium to high heat, heat a sauté pan and pour in oil, coating surface of pan. Add onion, garlic, and herbs, stirring with wooden spoon until brown, 6 to 8 minutes. Add to chile pods in blender. Add 4 cups of warm water and blend until smooth. Strain through sieve to remove any non-emulsified ingredients like seeds or stems.

EAST INDIAN SPINACH PUREE

8 cups spinach, rinsed and stemmed
3 tablespoons unsalted butter
1 onion, peeled and diced
3 tablespoons fresh chopped ginger
3 tablespoons fresh chopped garlic
1 teaspoon ground fenugreek
1 teaspoon ground cumin
½ teaspoon ground nutmeg
¼ teaspoon ground clove
¼ teaspoon cinnamon
1 cup cooked rice, preferably Texmati
4 cups heavy cream

1. Blanch the spinach leaves in salted boiling water for 2 minutes, rinse until cool, then drain. Set aside.
2. Melt butter in a large saucepan over medium-high heat, add onion, ginger, and garlic, and sauté for 5 minutes. Add all ground spices and toast for 2 minutes. Add spinach and rice and stir for 3 minutes. Add cream and bring to a high simmer. Let cool, then blend until smooth.

SUCCOTASH

3 tablespoons unsalted butter
2 zucchini, quartered and diced
2 summer squash, quartered and diced
1 large onion, peeled and diced
3 tablespoons fresh garlic, chopped
2 cups corn
1 cup green chile, diced
2 tablespoons dried oregano
1 tablespoon ground cumin
Salt and pepper to taste

1. Over medium heat in a large sauté pan, add butter to melt and coat pan. Add zucchini, squash, and onion and sauté for 3 minutes. Add garlic and stir for 2 minutes. Add corn and green chile and sauté for 3 minutes, stirring pan to avoid burning. Add oregano and cumin, sauté until brown, then set aside to cool. Salt and pepper to taste.

PUMPKIN, KALE, AND CHANTERELLE MUSHROOM FILLING

2 tablespoons unsalted butter
2 cups thinly sliced pumpkin
3 cups fresh chanterelle or porcini mushrooms
2 cups stemmed and chopped kale

1. Over medium heat in a large sauté pan, melt butter to coat pan. Add pumpkin and sauté until brown, 3 minutes. Add mushrooms and kale and sauté 3 to 5 minutes more, until kale is wilted and mushrooms are brown. Salt and pepper to taste.

GREEN RICE

1 jalapeño, seeded
1 cup cilantro
1 cup parsley
1 cup chives
4 cloves garlic
½ cup pure olive oil
2 cups cooked rice

1. Place all ingredients except oil and rice in blender and blend on medium speed. Add oil to form paste. Fold into warm cooked rice.

ASSEMBLY

12 corn tortillas
½ cup cotija cheese

1. Warm each component of dish.
2. Warm three 6-inch corn tortillas.
3. On serving plate, spoon a thin pool of spinach puree 7 inches in diameter around plate. Place one 6-inch tortilla on top of sauce.
4. Place ¼ cup of green rice on tortilla. Add ½ cup of succotash on top of rice. Place a second warm tortilla on top. Place ½ cup pumpkin, kale, and mushroom sauté on top.
4. Cover with the third warm tortilla.
5. Smother enchilada with red chile. Garnish with crumbled cotija cheese. Place under broiler until cheese browns and sauces bubble.

FLAN ATENCIO

El Paragua's Frances Atencio shared her famous flan recipe with us years ago. The Española restaurant has served hearty, home-cooked New Mexican cuisine for more than 50 years.

Serves 8 to 12

1¾ cups sugar, divided
3 eggs
5 egg yolks
2 13-ounce cans evaporated
 milk
2 teaspoons vanilla
6 tablespoons brandy or
 rum (optional)

1. Preheat oven to 350°. Put 1 cup of the sugar into a deep baking pan or loaf pan. Place over medium-high heat. Stirring constantly with a wooden spoon, melt sugar. When sugar turns golden brown, remove from heat and tilt pan so caramel evenly coats the inside. Let cool.
2. Meanwhile, beat eggs and yolks with remaining sugar, milk, and vanilla. Strain mixture into the caramel-coated pan. Cover with lid or foil. Place pan in a larger pan containing an inch of hot water. Bake for 1 hour. Let cool completely.
3. To serve, turn onto a serving platter. For a spectacular presentation, you could pour warmed brandy or rum over the custard and light it to send it to the table aflame.

CRANBERRY PECAN PIE

Adela Amador's "Southwest Flavor" column for *New Mexico Magazine* ran from 1993 to 2006, mixing recipes with memories of her life in New Mexico. She liked to make this pie for the holidays because the cranberries "offer a nice contrast to the sweetness of pecan pie and add a touch of color." It tastes even better when you use New Mexico pecans.

1 9-inch unbaked pie crust
1 cup fresh cranberries, chopped
3 eggs
1 cup dark corn syrup
⅔ cup sugar
4 tablespoons (½ stick) butter, melted
½ teaspoon cinnamon
⅛ teaspoon nutmeg
1 cup pecan halves

1. Preheat oven to 325°. Place pie crust in pan and flute edges as desired, or press with fork to decorate edges. Sprinkle cranberries on top of crust.
2. In a medium bowl, beat eggs with corn syrup, sugar, butter, cinnamon, and nutmeg until mixture is well blended but not foamy. Pour over cranberries in crust. Carefully arrange pecan halves in a series of circles over the filling.
3. Bake for 50 to 55 minutes, or until a knife inserted in the center comes out clean. Be sure not to overbake the filling. The pie might still jiggle a little when the knife comes out clean, but it will firm up. This pie is especially good served chilled with sweetened whipped cream.

TRADITIONAL TAMALES
WITH RED CHILE BEEF FILLING

Jane Butel introduced New Mexico cooking to the world through her many cookbooks, television appearances, and Jane Butel's Southwest Cooking School, in Albuquerque. This recipe for a traditional New Mexico holiday classic was her mother's all-time favorite recipe for tamales. They're delicious served with red chile sauce.

Makes 4 to 5 dozen tamales

FILLING

1½ pounds beef stew meat, cut into chunks
Beef bouillon or broth
1½ tablespoons butter or bacon drippings
½ teaspoon garlic (1 clove), minced
½ cup ground pure red chile (hot chile is
   generally preferred)
¾ teaspoon salt
¼ teaspoon ground Mexican oregano

1. Simmer the meat in beef bouillon or broth, covering the meat by at least an inch. Cover the pot and cook meat until tender. Reserve broth. Cut the meat into very small cubes or chop in a food processor. In a heavy skillet, lightly brown the meat in the butter or bacon drippings.

2. After the meat has browned a bit, add the garlic and cook for about 2 minutes. Remove pan from heat, cool slightly, and add the ground chile. Season with salt and oregano. Add only enough broth to create a thick mixture and simmer the sauce uncovered, stirring regularly until thick and smooth— about 15 minutes.

MASA (CORNMEAL MIXTURE)

3½ cups warm water
6 cups masa harina (yellow, white, or blue)
2 cups lard
1¾ teaspoons salt

1. Add the warm water to the masa harina to make a very thick mixture that holds together, then let it stand. After a few minutes, begin drizzling in cold water, mixing well to prevent lumps, until the mixture is the consistency of pudding. Allow to set for at least 5 minutes. Add more cold water if needed.

2. Just before rolling the tamales, using the high speed on an electric mixer, cream the lard with the salt until very fluffy; it will float on water. Combine the lard with the masa using the lowest speed on an electric mixer. Mix only until well blended.

CORN HUSKS

6 to 7 dozen corn husks, soaked in warm water
Hot water

1. Soak the corn husks in hot water until soft and pliable. Start this step before preparing the masa and the filling. Pull strips off about a dozen husks to use for tying the tamales.

2. Spread about 2 tablespoons of masa mixture on each softened corn husk, making a rectangle about 3 by 4 inches and leaving at least a 2-inch margin of husk around the edges. Next, place about a tablespoon of the meat filling in a strip down the center of each tamale, being careful not to place too much filling.

3. Roll the husk sides in, then either twist both ends and tie them with strips of corn husk, or fold bottom up and top down and tie together in the center. If you plan to freeze the tamales, do so at this point, before steaming them later.

4. In a large pot that can be used for conventional steaming, or in a pressure cooker, pour ¾ inch of water in the bottom. Stand the tamales upright on a rack in the pot or cooker. Steam the tamales in a pot for 45 minutes, or in a pressure cooker under 15 pounds of pressure for 20 minutes. Serve with red chile sauce.

Note: Any leftover masa or meat mixture can be frozen. The steamed tamales can also be frozen. Each can be frozen for up to a year.

EMPANADITAS

These fruit pies, smaller than empanadas, are a big hit at special occasions, including Christmas and Pueblo feast days. At the Trujillo Family Farm, on Nambé Pueblo, Gloria Trujillo and her family grow chile, squash, and corn that regularly earn blue ribbons from the New Mexico State Fair. The Trujillos are equally known for their empanaditas, gathering to make hundreds for friends, neighbors, and family feasts. This is their famous recipe, which appeared in *New Mexico Magazine*'s December 1995 issue. A Spanish colonial version of the recipe calls for the pies to be filled with mincemeat and fried.

Makes 10

DOUGH

1½ cups flour
1 teaspoon baking powder
½ teaspoon salt
6 tablespoons lard or vegetable
   shortening, chilled

FILLING

1 cup dried fruit, cooked, drained,
   and chopped (apricots,
   peaches, pears, raisins, or
   prunes)
Additional sweetening, if needed:
   ⅓ cup sugar or 1 tablespoon
   honey
¼ teaspoon ground cinnamon
1 egg
1 tablespoon milk

1. Pour boiling water over dried fruit and let sit until softened, then strain.
2. Preheat oven to 400°. Combine flour, baking powder, and salt in a mixing bowl. Cut in lard until mixture resembles fine meal. Slowly add water until dough is easy to roll. Roll out to ¼-inch thickness and cut into 4-inch rounds.
3. Stir the chopped fruit, sweetening, and cinnamon together and put 1 tablespoon of filling on one half of each round. Fold over the other half of the round and pinch the edges together firmly. Prick the tops in several places using the tines of a fork. Mix the egg with the milk and brush the tops of the pies. Bake for 15 minutes, or until lightly browned.

NATILLAS

HOLIDAY FAVORITE

Traditional natillas are a creamy custard lightened with beaten egg whites, in the style of "floating island" desserts. This recipe, published in our October 2012 issue, comes from the family of Pete and Eligia Torres, who founded Pete's Café, in Belén, in 1949. Locals and tourists alike can't get enough of this renowned restaurant's authentic New Mexico cuisine.

Serves 6 to 8

4 cups (1 quart) half-and-half, divided
1 cup sugar, divided
Dash of salt
3 large eggs, separated
⅓ cup all-purpose flour
1 teaspoon pure vanilla extract

1. Combine 3 cups half-and-half, ¾ cup sugar, and salt in heavy saucepan and warm over medium heat.
2. While mixture warms, whisk together egg yolks, flour, and remaining cup half-and-half. When saucepan mixture comes to a boil, let it bubble away for 2 minutes. Remove from heat and pour egg yolk mixture through fine strainer or sieve into saucepan, stirring constantly. Return saucepan to medium heat and bring custard gradually to a boil again, stirring frequently. Simmer 8 to 10 minutes, until custard is thick enough to moderately coat spoon.
3. Remove from heat and stir in vanilla.
4. Custard can be served warm or refrigerated for up to several hours, which will thicken it a bit. Before serving, beat egg whites and remaining ¼ cup sugar with electric mixer until peaks form. Fold egg white mixture into custard and serve.

HOLIDAY HOT CHOCOLATE

Make a memorable toast to the holidays with this spirit-warming elixir from well-known Santa Fe chef Rocky Durham, who contributed this recipe to our February 2011 issue. Hot chocolate has never tasted so scrumptious, thanks to New Mexico red chile and a host of holiday spices. ¡Salud!

Makes about 3 cups

1 2-ounce tablet Mexican
   chocolate (such as Ibarra)
½ teaspoon cinnamon
½ teaspoon aniseed
½ teaspoon black pepper
½ teaspoon cumin
½ teaspoon coriander
½ teaspoon allspice
½ teaspoon nutmeg
1 tablespoon hot New Mexican red
   chile powder
2 tablespoons blue cornmeal
2½ cups milk or half-and-half
4 tablespoons agave nectar
Pinch of salt

1. Using the coarse side of a box grater, grate chocolate tablets.
2. Place all ground spices in a sauté pan over medium heat. Stirring frequently, toast spices until slightly darker and aromatic. Add chile powder and toast 1 minute more, stirring constantly. Remove spices from pan and set aside.
3. In small saucepan, toast cornmeal over medium heat until aromatic, 3 to 4 minutes, stirring frequently. Add milk or half-and-half and whisk to combine thoroughly.
4. Add all the other ingredients to the milk. Bring to a simmer, stirring occasionally. Adjust seasonings to taste and serve in warm mugs.

BIZCOCHITOS

These cookies not only are the official New Mexico state cookie; they're also a favorite at the popular Cornerstone Bakery & Cafe, in Ruidoso. They're light, crispy, and filled with a licorice-like flavor in every bite, thanks to the traditional addition of anise. You'll want to bake a bushel of these bizcochitos as holiday gifts for family and friends, and don't forget yourself.

Makes about 100 cookies

3 pounds lard
2 pounds and 3½ ounces granulated sugar
2 tablespoons aniseed
6 large eggs
¾ cup brandy
6 pounds and 4¼ ounces all-purpose flour
¾ teaspoon salt
3 tablespoons baking powder
Cinnamon sugar for dusting

1. In a large mixing bowl, cream together lard, sugar, and aniseed until evenly incorporated. Add eggs and brandy; cream until smooth. Add flour, salt, and baking powder. Mix until a dough is formed. Roll into a log and wrap in plastic. Chill in the fridge for at least 2 hours.

2. On a lightly floured surface, roll out the dough to a little more than ¼ inch thick. Cut into a cookie shape. (The Cornerstone bakers use a 3¼-inch-diameter round cutter.)

3. Set cookies flat on a parchment-lined sheet pan in rows. Dust with cinnamon sugar.

4. Bake at 350° for 10 minutes, until light golden brown. Let cool completely and enjoy! These are best stored in an airtight container.

THE BELOVED BIZCOCHITO

In 1989, New Mexico became the first state to declare an official state cookie, despite a humorous legislature floor debate over how to spell it. Bizcochito or biscochito? Linguists say either one works. Besides, cookies are for biting, not fighting. Juliette C de Baca wrote rhapsodically of the melt-in-your-mouth morsels in a December 1966 article, "Christmas Is Biscochitos":

"In New Mexico, Christmas will always mean biscochitos ... And what exactly is a biscochito? Oh, amigos, how can you describe a snowflake? Or the aroma of a piñon fire? Or the kiss of a beautiful morenita? For a biscochito is a blessing that the good Lord has chosen to give the people of this lovely land of poco tiempo ... To really enjoy biscochitos, amigos, one should have some vino or chocolate. Not the usual American chocolate, but the thick, rich, spicy chocolate beaten until it has a deep foam and served with a dust of cinnamon ... One bite of those delicate little cakes would make anyone forget ... the cares of the world."

RECIPE NOTES

Subscribe to

Founded in 1923, New Mexico Magazine has been the authoritative guide to exploring
the state's diverse people, food, culture, arts, shopping, and outdoor recreation for 100 years.

newmexicomagazine.org/subscribe